THE ENGLI

TRIFLE

Trifle, based on an illustration in Mrs Beeton, 1861.

THE ENGLISH KITCHEN

TRIFLE

Helen Saberi

AND

Alan Davidson

PROSPECT BOOKS

2009

Published in this form in 2009 by Prospect Books,
Allaleigh House, Blackawton, Totnes, Devon TQ9 7DL.

Trifle was first published by Prospect Books in 2001.

BRITISH LIBRARY CATALOGUING IN PUBLICATION DATA:
A catalogue entry for this book is available from the British
Library.

ISBN 978-1-903018-72-9

The cover is the composition 'Trifle' by Ali Roscoe. The photograph
taken by Clare Pawley.

Those illustrations in the text which are based on material from
Mrs Beeton and Theodore Garrett are by James Stewart.

Typeset in Hoefler Text by Tom Jaine.

Printed and bound in Great Britain by the Cromwell Press Group,
Trowbridge, Wiltshire.

ACKNOWLEDGEMENTS

Our first thanks go to our respective spouses, Jane Davidson and Nasir Saberi, both of whom have been called on to tolerate invasions of kitchen space by great clutters of ingredients and equipment for testing recipes, and whose comments have been consistently helpful.

Next we thank our publisher Tom Jaine, for encouraging our project and waiting with great patience for the little book to be completed.

Many other people have given us valuable help. Some kindly sent us recipes; some graciously allowed us to reproduce recipes or texts of which they had the copyright and some provided pertinent information and helpful ideas. Their generosity has been remarkable and is evidence of how strongly the subject of Trifles appeals to all. Here is a list of these kind people, with our warm thanks to all of them for their support, given in many and various ways. We also express our gratitude to all the other authors mentioned in the text, or the bibliography, as sources of inspiration or practical information.

Myrtle Allen, James Bishop, Shirley Lomax Brooks, Catherine Brown, Ann and Helen Caruana Galizia, Lesley Chamberlain, Jack Conte, Ivan Day, Fuchsia Dunlop, Ove Fosså, Svein Fosså, Brenda Garza Sada, Sophie Grigson, Hilary Hyman, Philip and Mary Hyman, Phil Iddison, Peter James-Smith, Tom Johnstone and the Estate of F. Marian McNeill,[*] Maria Kaneva-Johnson, Rachel Laudan, Helen Leach, Gilly Lehmann, Margaret Little, Fiona Lucraft, John Mariani, Laura Mason, Jill Norman, Mary Norwak, Henry Notaker, Marguerite Patten, Chris Payne, Alicia Rios, Nanna Rögnvaldardóttir, Françoise Sabban, Barbara Santich, Marta Scheffer, Ann Semple, Regina Sexton, Catherine (Sheridan) Tingley, Maria Dolores Torres Yzábal, Olivia Warren.

[*] In expressing our thanks to the Estate, we are asked to point out that the current (Mercat Press) edition of Marian McNeill's *The Scots Kitchen* (see page 53), is a facsimile of the first 1929 edition, so does not contain the recipe which we have taken from the 1963 edition.

FAST TRACK GUIDE

There are over ninety recipes for trifle in this book, some of them included for historical reasons or as curiosities. Readers who are simply looking for something practical (or, alternatively, for something really exotic or challenging) can use this 'fast track guide' to recipes likely to suit them.

QUICK AND EASY

1. May Byron's Countess Trifle, p. 41
2. Danish Raspberry Foam, p. 83
3. Grape and Ginger Syllabub, p. 104
4. Ratafia Trifle, p. 46

TRADITIONAL AND GUARANTEED TO PRODUCE A GOOD RESULT

1. Marian McNeill's Scots Trifle, p. 53
2. Jane Grigson's Banana Trifle, p. 56
3. Icelandic Ommutriffli, p. 85
4. Easter Trifle, p. 43

SPECIALLY FESTIVE

1. *PPC* Celebration Trifle, p. 61
2. Caramelized Orange trifle, p. 59
3. Trifle Belle Hélène, p. 58
4. Summer Syllabub, p. 58
5. A Sicilian Zuppa Inglese, p. 107

REALLY EXOTIC

1. Ante de Yemas, p. 75
2. Viceroy's Dessert, p. 76
3. Eritrean Trifle, p. 90
4. Kabul Trifle, p. 112
5. Vientiane Trifle, p. 113

TABLE OF CONTENTS

This attractive drawing by Juliet Stanwell Smith served as the keynote illustration for the chapter on 'Tipsy Cakes and Trifles' in Mary Norwak's charming and authoritative book English Puddings, Sweet and Savoury *(Batsford, London, 1981). Reproduced here by kind permission of Mary Norwak, it serves equally well to complement the Introduction to our own book, by displaying in an English countryside setting a panoply of members of the trifle family (including a baked trifle on the left, what are probably whim-whams at the back, a tipsy cake hedgehog on the right, and of course a mainstream traditional trifle in the foreground).*

INTRODUCTION

Preparing this book has been a delightful experience for both of us. During the long years when we were toiling away together on the massive *Oxford Companion to Food* we often thought how refreshing it would be, when that was finished, to switch to some small, light project. And what better topic for this than the trifle, 'a thing of no consequence', 'something light and frothy'.

The project had its pilot: a major essay, introduced by Alan, which Helen contributed to the special 50th issue of the journal *PPC*. A quotation from what each of us wrote then will show with what lively interest we approached the subject.

ALAN OBSERVED THAT: 'One of the great paradoxes of culinary terminology is that what many people see as Britain's supreme contribution to the dessert tables of the world, for children and adults alike, to wit the trifle, should bear a name which suggests that it is of no consequence. This, surely, is carrying much too far the British tradition of playing down the merits of things British.' Urging that due tribute should be made to this essentially British confection, he added that: 'in cottage and castle alike this plebeian yet aristocratic, complex yet simple, creation achieves a degree of satisfaction for human appetites and an aesthetic and emotional impact which stand unrivalled on the tablecloth.'

HELEN WROTE: 'Trifles offer a rare combination of sensual and intellectual pleasures. How many times have I dipped my spoon into one and experienced in succession the light frothy cream, the smooth velvety custard, the tangy fruit mingling with the bouquet of wine (or sherry or liqueur), and perhaps a touch of almondy crunchiness from ratafias or macaroons, and lastly the sweet, soft but crumbly texture of the sponge or sponge fingers. Mmm, the very thought sets me off. But this literal dipping of the spoon can be matched on the intellectual side by delving into the successive layers of the history of the trifle, with a pleasure almost as intense. ... I have made trifle many times over many years and always with real enjoyment – a trifle with its carousel of flavours, colours and textures is so easy to make.'

With this twofold testimony to our enthusiasm, we introduce this book, a real labour of love. In it we seek not only to provide a panoply of well tested recipes (ah, happy days when we had two trifles a week to sample and discuss over lunch!), and to describe the history and essential nature of the trifle in its homeland, but also to exhibit relations of the trifle in other continents, showing the degree of biodiversity which this dish has achieved.

Diversity? Yes, we know that *The New Shorter Oxford English Dictionary* defines the current meaning of trifle, in a culinary context, quite precisely and narrowly: 'Now a dessert of sponge cake (esp. flavoured with sherry or spirit) with custard, jelly, fruit, whipped cream etc.' But in fact variations on the trifle theme – all delicious – seem to us to be just about as infinite as the stars in the sky. And we should not overlook the last word of the *NSOED* definition. That little 'etc.' covers a multitude of things (yes, 'hundreds and thousands' one might say, if tempted by a play on words).

Now, we wish our readers as much pleasure in using the book and eating trifles as we have had in preparing the book (and of course eating trifles ourselves). The pleasure for us was all the greater, because, thanks to the generosity of Jane Davidson, we were able to compose the book in ideal surroundings, a courtyard complex in Chelsea, built in 1885 by Elijah Hoole to provide accommodation and a garden for 60 labourers. The driving force behind the project was Lady Kate Courtney (died 1929, after many decades of beneficent activities in Chelsea). It is to her memory that we dedicate this book.

Alan Davidson and Helen J. Saberi
The Porticos, King's Road, Chelsea
December 2000

USING THE RECIPES

All the recipes have been carefully tested, except for certain old ones which are given verbatim from the original source. We felt that in many instances readers would prefer just to see for themselves what, say, Mrs Raffald wrote in the eighteenth century, without the comments, substitutions and adaptations which are the almost inevitable result of testing.

It is difficult to think of any trifle recipe whose instructions should be treated as sacrosanct. Almost all contain ingredients which can be substituted by something else without detriment.

- Thus 'sponge cake' takes many forms, any of which will do, and other plain cake may be just as effective.
- No-one need feel bound to use Madeira wine if it is more convenient to use Malaga or Sherry.
- A specified fruit or jam can often be replaced by another (peach for apricot, strawberry for raspberry), although it would be inappropriate to use a substitute for gooseberry or banana if these fruits were principal ingredients.
- The whole field of decorations (candied petals, angelica, hundreds and thousands, etc.) for the top of a trifle is wide open to whatever variations appeal. Thickness of layers, amounts of whipped cream or syllabub, dosage of an alcoholic drink (if used), etc. – all may be varied.

A table of equivalent weights and measures is provided at the end of the book. This provides only the information which is relevant to the recipes in this book. Here again, flexibility is in order. For example, if a recipe calls for 'cups', you can normally use either Imperial or American, so long as you stick to one kind of cup throughout any given recipe. The same applies to pints.

In choosing a recipe, readers may find it especially helpful to consult the Fast Track Guide (p. 6) and to browse through the Table of Contents, specially enhanced for this purpose. Readers who still find difficulty in choosing among our ninety or so recipes may like to reflect on the difficulties we had in choosing from the many hundreds we have examined.

TRIFLE ARCHITECTURE

The construction of a trifle – anyway, a trifle on a domestic scale – does not call for the use of cranes or excavators and mechanical spreaders, but it does exemplify the application of some principles which apply to the construction of buildings.

As with a building, so with a trifle – the foundations are very important. Where the building would be set on compacted rubble, the trifle starts at the bottom with its layer of moist compacted sponge (and macaroons or whatever), bound by jam to prevent disconcerting shifts as the weight above is increased. For those who admit a layer of jelly, this will replace the uneven surface of the 'rubble' with a solid sheet of load-bearing substance – the counterpart of a screeded concrete floor. Otherwise a custard which has set firmly will fill this role, instead of sitting on top of the jelly.

In this connection, and on the assumption that the top of the trifle is to be decorated, then special attention must be paid to the loadbearing capacity of the topping, for example, the whipped cream or syllabub. There are many variables here, of which the trifle decorator should be mindful. One is the 'footprint' of any given piece of decoration. If this is very small, as in the case of one of the tiny 'hundreds and thousands' which are sometimes used, then it will penetrate the topping at a relatively high speed, even if its weighs little. If, on the other hand, the footprint is quite large, as in the case of a thin flat strip of candied angelica, it will stay in place for longer. Candied flower petals are quite good in this respect, and they also have an advantage in being very light weight. To state the obvious, the heavier a decoration is the faster it will sink. Another variable is the stiffness of the whipped cream (or whatever); the stiffer the better for holding up decorations. The depth of the layer of whipped cream and the diameter of the bowl are also relevant; take special care if the depth is very great. And, since the ambient temperature will also have an effect, chill a decorated trifle before serving.

CHAPTER ONE

THE EARLY YEARS

It would be pleasant to think that it was a contemporary of Shakespeare, and the author of what has been described as the finest Tudor cookery book, who was the first to bring into print a recipe for making a trifle, that most English (or rather British) of sweet and festive dishes. And so it would seem. Thomas Dawson, author of the book in question (*The Good Huswife's Iewell*, 1596) gives a recipe which is clearly headed 'To make a Trifle'. However, his text, which is reproduced below, does not describe anything like the trifle which has been familiar to us for well over two centuries, but seems rather to be a recipe for a Fool (see the Glossary).

To make a Trifle

Take a pinte of thicke Creame, and season it with Sugar and Ginger, and Rosewater, so stirre it as you would then have it, and make it luke warme in a dish on a Chafingdish and coals, and after put it into a silver piece or bowle, and so serve it to the boorde.

What little is known about Dawson, and the speculations which have plausibly been made by Maggie Black (in her introduction to the 1996 edition of his book) suggest that he was a man of considerable gifts, well practised in kitchen arts even if not a professional cook. It may therefore be taken as definite that at the end of the sixteenth century something called trifle but more like a fool did exist. This is supported by the *NSOED* which tells us that originally in the late sixteenth century, the culinary meaning of the word trifle was 'a dish composed of cream, boiled with various ingredients', i.e. not far removed from what we call a fool, which nowadays is usually a fruit purée and cream combined. Indeed Florio, in his dictionary of 1598, bracketed the two terms when he wrote: 'a kind of clouted cream called a foole or a trifle.'

Books which appeared in the seventeenth century and the early part of the eighteenth corroborate this. The fool/trifle seems to have been an established item for nearly two centuries. The convergence of the two terms at that time is well exemplified in the next book on our list, *The Art of Cookery Refin'd* by Jos Cooper, dated 1654 and of exceptional interest for reasons explained by Louise A. Richardson and J.R. Isabell (1984). His recipe is entitled 'To make a Foole', although in fact it comes a little closer, by incorporation of slices of bread at the bottom of the dish, to the modern trifle.

To make a Foole

Slice a Manchet [loaf of fine bread] very thin and lay it in the bottom of a dish; and wet them with Sack; boyle Creame, with Eggs, and three or foure blades of Mace; season it with Rosewater and Sugar, stir it well together to prevent curdling; then pour it on the Bread and let it coole; then serve it up to the Table.

Many more examples could be given from later authors including Hannah Woolley, in *The Lady's Closet* (or *Queen-Like Closet*) of 1672 (5th edn. 1684). Her recipe does illustrate two new developments. It includes rennet; which produces a 'set' rather than a liquid confection. It is also the first trifle recipe to provide for using comfits (see Glossary).

To make a Trifle

Take Sweet Cream, season it with Rosewater and Sugar, and a little whole Mace, let it boil a while, then take it off, and let it cool, and when it is lukewarm put it into such little Dishes or Bowls as you mean to serve it in; then put in a little Runnet, and stir it together; when you serve it in, strew on some French Comfits.

One of the most famous Englishmen of the seventeenth century, John Evelyn, also had a recipe for this sort of 'trifle', which appears in the collection of his manuscript recipes edited by Christopher Driver.

A trife

Take some creame and boyle it with Cinnamon and mace
take out the spice when it is boyled sweeten the cream with
some fine sugar put in a spoonful or 2 of Rose water and
when it is allmost cold put in as much rennet as will bring
it to a tender curd.

And Robert May, whose book *The Accomplisht Cook* (1685 edn.) is the
finest and fullest cookery work of the century, conforms.

Triffel

Take a quart of the best and thickest cream, set it on the fire
in a clean skillet, and put to it whole mace, cinnamon, and
sugar, boil it well in the cream before you put in the sugar;
then your cream being well boiled, pour it into a fine silver
piece or dish, and take out the spices, let it cool till it be
no more than blood-warm, then put in a spoonful of good
runnet, and set it well together being cold scrape sugar on
it, and trim the dish sides finely.

Mrs Mary Eales (1718), the self-proclaimed 'Confectioner to the late
Queen Anne', has a trifle which is similar to May's, except that she
adds orange flower water instead of cinnamon and mace; and she
says specifically, after the rennet had been put in, 'let it stand 'till it
comes like Cheese'. This gives a clear impression of the consistency
which a trifle was expected to have in that time.

To make a TRIFLE

Take a Pint of Cream, and boil it, and when it is almost cold,
sweeten it, and put it in the Bason you use it in; and put to it
a Spoonful of Runnet; let it stand 'till it comes like Cheese:
You may perfume it, or put in Orange-Flower-Water.

So far as we can ascertain, the prescription of Mrs Eales was
followed by three decades of silence. Yet it was during these three
decades that someone, somewhere, created what we know as a trifle
and, perhaps for lack of a better alternative, transferred to it the
name which had for so long belonged to a category of fools.

To make a TRIFLE.

TAKE a Pint of Cream, and boil it, and when it is almoſt cold, ſweeten it, and put it in the Baſon you uſe it in; and put to it a Spoonful of Runnet; let it ſtand 'till it comes like Cheeſe : You may perfume it, or put in Orange-Flower-Water.

A facsimile of Mrs Mary Eales's receipt for trifle, the edition of 1733.

CHAPTER TWO

BRITISH TRIFLES
1750–1800

It is 1751, and the world will never be the same again, not anyway for British cooks and party-givers and dessert-lovers. The fourth edition of Hannah Glasse's famous book *The Art of Cookery Made Plain and Easy* has just been published and so has the fifth edition of the important book which began life as *The Whole Duty of a Woman* in 1737 but acquired a new title, *The Lady's Companion* in later editions. There, in these two publications, without fanfare but staring everyone in the face, were the first printed recipes for a real trifle.

Hannah Glasse's recipe

It would be a fine example of irony if Hannah, notorious for the ruthless way in which she plagiarized earlier authors (see Jennifer Stead, 1983, Priscilla Bain, 1986, and Fiona Lucraft, 1997, 1998) had in fact, this once, invented something. In default of any evidence to the contrary, she must have the benefit of the doubt and be hailed for her feat.

Feat it surely was. To leap from the fool-trifle to the modern trifle was to cross a wide chasm, so wide that one is tempted to think, as a biologist would, that there must have been a 'missing link'. Possibly this could have been the Floating Island, which does have some of the characteristics which one would have expected in any intermediate dish. Here again, Hannah Glasse seems to have been the first to put this into print, in the first edition of her book (1747).

Here, anyway, are Hannah's two recipes, in temporal sequence, so that readers may judge for themselves.

The Flooting Island, *a pretty Dish for the Middle of a Table at a Second Course, or for Supper* (1747)

Take a Soop Dish according to the Size and Quantity you would make; but a pretty deep Glass Dish is best, and set it on a China Dish, first take a Quart of the thickest Cream you can get, make it pretty sweet with fine Sugar, pour in a Gill of Sack, grate the yellow Rind of a Lemon in, and mill the Cream till it is all of a thick Froth, then as carefully as you can, pour the thin from the Froth into a Dish; take a French Role [brioche-type roll], or as many as you want, cut it as thin as you can, lay a Layer of that as light as possible on the Cream, then a Layer of Currant-jelly, then a very thin Layer of Role, and then Hartshorn-jelly, then French Role, and over that whip your Froth which you saved off the Cream very well milled up, and lay at Top as high as you can heap it; and as for the Rim of the Dish set it round with Fruit or Sweetmeats according to your Fancy, this looks very pretty in the middle of a Table with Candles round it, and you may make it of as many different Colours as you fancy, and according to what Jellies and Giams, or Sweet-meats you have; or at the Bottom of your Dish you may put the thickest Cream you can get; but that is as you fancy.

To make a Trifle (1751)

Cover the Bottom of your Dish or Bowl with Naples Biscuits, broke in Pieces, Mackeroons broke in Halves, and Ratafia Cakes. Just wet them all through with Sack, then make a good boiled Custard, not too thick, and when cold pour over it, then put a Syllabub over that. You may garnish it with Ratifia Cakes, Currant Jelly and Flowers.

The Floating Island recipe, in particular, is so full and colourful that it creates an impression of Hannah really being enthusiastic about this sort of thing. Incidentally, we applaud what she says about having any colours you fancy and about the effect of having lighted candles around the dish – advice very much in tune with our own feelings.

Certainly, Hannah followed up her first trifle with something grander, to wit the recipe for 'A Grand Trifle' which appeared in her *Compleat Confectioner* of *c.* 1760, see page 24.

We can only speculate whether publication of Hannah Glasse's first trifle recipe in 1751 resulted in lots of cooks starting to make trifles her way. However, there are two interesting pieces of evidence.

First, the author Beverley Nichols acquired in the 1930s a cookery manuscript which he found in romantic circumstances in a more or less hidden little cupboard in a cottage in the hamlet of Glatton in Huntingdonshire. This was published in 1968 in a book called *In an Eighteenth Century Kitchen* with an introduction by Nichols and a scholarly commentary by Dr Dennis Rhodes, from which we may infer that when the manuscript has a date beside a recipe, that was the date when the recipe was written in. Some of them are attributed to ladies such as 'Sister Mason'. In the first section of the manuscript, the outstanding contributor is 'Mrs Powell', who provides four recipes, all with the date 1752 beside them; and one of these is the trifle recipe reproduced below:

1752   MRS POWELL   WAY TO MAKE A TRIFLE
Take savoy biskakes dip Them in sack & lay Them in the bottom (allmost double) of a Cheney [China] dish Then Take a pint of Cream & make a custard with four egg boil The Custard & pour it on The bistcakes : Then Take a pint of Cream & make a whipt sillybub & put it on the Custard. N.B. when you eat it put your spoon into The Bottom of The dish.

The high degree of compatibility between Hannah Glasse's recipe and Mrs Powell's could lead to interesting speculations: is it possible that one was derived from the other? If Mrs Powell already had the recipe some years before it got copied into the manuscript (and this is a perfectly reasonable supposition), then could Hannah Glasse have got it from Mrs Powell and rewritten it somewhat to match her own style? The fact that a 'Mr Powel' was among subscribers to the first edition of Hannah Glasse's book is suggestive, but more detective work would be needed to go into the matter properly.

The second piece of evidence is more exciting. Our publisher has in his possession a copy of a trifle recipe, of the modern sort, from an old manuscript recipe book; and it bears the date May the 8th, 1750. It is attributed to 'Sister Nanny'. The book, whose compiler is unknown, is thought to belong to Devon.

A trifle

Lay some Savoy biscuits at the bottom of the dish Wet them with white wine Lay a custard over them until the dish is full but let the custard be cold before it be put on the biscuit Then on the custard a whipped syllabub as much as you can to make it high.

This is the earliest written recipe for our sort of trifle which has so far come to light. Here again, more detective work is called for, to establish the identity of Sister Nanny. Although her recipe is also compatible with Hannah Glasse's, and indeed with Mrs Powell's, they are far removed from each other in wording.

THE LADY'S COMPANION RECIPES

As mentioned above, *The Lady's Companion*, one of the great recipe compilations of the eighteenth century, had begun life as *The Whole Duty of a Woman* in 1737: a volume of almost 700 pages distinguished by a beautiful typography and by an introduction of 100 pages addressed to 'the fair sex; containing rules, directions, and observations, for their conduct and behaviour through all ages and circumstances of life, as virgins, wives, or widows' (no other forms of existence were envisaged). Although this introduction, so incorrect by modern standards, is written in a lively style and with some humour, the main function of the book was to provide hundreds and hundreds of recipes, at that time the largest collection ever formed in English. And in subsequent editions the 'duty of a woman' aspect was quietly downplayed, while the number of recipes grew and grew. It was in 1751 that the fifth, expanded, edition of this massive work first provided any guidance on making trifles; there had been none in the fourth edition of 1743. In fact, there were two recipes in the 1751 edition, reading thus:

To make a Trifle

Take a Quarter of a Pound of *Naples* Biscuits, put them in a deep *China* Dish, with as much Red Wine as they will take to soak them; smooth them with the back Part of a Spoon, then whip Half a Pint of Cream, as for a Syllabub with Sugar, lemon-juice, and a Spoonful of White Wine, and lay on the Froth by Spoonfuls till covered thick. If it dont froth stiff, add the Whites of two Eggs. You may garnish, when you serve it, with Apples, peeled Walnuts, or any Fruit that is in Season, as you like.

Another Way

Take the same Quantity of Biscuits as in the above Reciept, and place them as before directed; then warm Half a Pint of Sack or Red Wine, which you like, and pour over them; then take a Quart of Custard-stuff, made hot and put to them; then whip a Pint of Cream, or Milk, and lay on it by Spoonfuls till all the Cream is in.

It may be possible eventually to determine in what months the two publications of 1751 took place, and which of the two books can claim to have provided the first printed recipe for a trifle as we know it. Since Hannah Glasse, in her book, had plagiarized quite extensively an earlier edition of *The Lady's Companion*, it might seem tempting to speculate that again in 1751 she borrowed from the rival publication. But her recipe and those in *The Lady's Companion* are not similar.

FURTHER DEVELOPMENTS

Hannah Glasse's 'A grand trifle', in her book *The Compleat Confectioner* of 1760, is also intriguing. Is this the first time a jelly is the base of a trifle? It would seem so, and this point is of some significance in connection with a question which has intermittently and sometimes heatedly been debated in recent times, namely: is the use of jelly in a trifle sanctioned by tradition and permissible, or is it a vulgar solecism such as purists should eschew?

We have not been able to trace any other references to matrimony cakes, but they were clearly of a kind with Naples biscuits, etc. Mention of the King's table in the recipe serves as a reminder that it was in 1760 that George III succeeded George II, continuing the Hanoverian dynasty which had been established in 1714. Indeed it was under a German monarchy that the English trifle blossomed.

Anyway, here is Hannah Glasse's recipe:

A grand trifle

Take a very large china dish or glass; that is deep, first make some very fine rich calves-foot jelly, with which fill the dish about half the depth; when it begins to jelly, have ready some Naples biscuits, macaroons, and the little cakes called matrimony; take an equal quantity of these cakes, break them in pieces, and stick them in the jelly before it be stiff, all over very thick; pour over that a quart of very thick sweet cream, then lay all round, currant jelly, rasberry jam, and some calves-foot jelly, all cut in little pieces, with which garnish your dish thick all round, intermixing them and on them lay macaroons, and the little cakes, being first dipped in scak [sack].

Then take two quarts of the thickest cream you can get, sweeten it with double-refined sugar, grate into it the rine of three fine large lemons, and whisk it up with a whisk; take off the froth as it rises, and lay it in your dish as high as you can possibly raise it; this is fit to go to the King's table, if well made, and very excellent when it comes to be all mixed together.

The 1750s were indeed the decade of the trifle, and not only in England. North of the Border, Elizabeth Cleland (*A New and Easy Method of Cookery*) published in 1755 an engagingly Scottish recipe for trifle, into the text of which we have inserted explanations of Scottish terms which she used and the references she made to her other recipe, Yellow Cream (which in turn connects up with her recipe for Floating Island).

To make a Trifle

Cover your ashet [platter, from the French assiette] with Spunge Biscuits; then pour over them a Mutchkin [a Scottish measure, a little more than 400 ml] of Malaga, or white Wine, then a yellow Cream [which is made with cream, egg yolks, cinnamon, orange rind, to be eaten cold]; then lay on it Heaps of coloured Sweet-meats; roast six or seven Apples, and rub them through a Search [variant of 'searce', meaning sieve, strainer]; put a little Sugar to them, and mix them with four Eggs, the Whites only, and wipe them up very high, and put this by Spoonfuls over the rest; but let a little of the Cream and Sweet-meats be seen. Raise it up as high as you can so send it to the Table.

Returning to England we find that Martha Bradley, whose *The British Housewife* (*c.* 1758) is one of the two or three greatest English cookery books of the eighteenth century, has a good trifle recipe, here followed by a detail from the frontispiece of her book:

A Trifle.

Break into a large Bowl some Naples Biscuits, Macaroons, and Ratafia Cakes; cover the Bottom of the Bowl with these, and pour over them as much Sack as will just wet them through.

Make a boiled Custard, but moderately thick; set it by to cool, and when quite cold pour it over them; then pour in a Syllabub over that, and garnish with Currant Jelly and Ratafia Cakes.

However, although Martha Bradley's recipe is a good one, Elizabeth Raffald in *The Experienced English Housekeeper* (we refer to the third edition of 1773) has those little extra touches which we all recognize when we see them, which give us a 'real feel' for how a dish is made:

To make a Trifle

PUT three large maccaroons in the middle of your dish, pour as much white wine over them as they will drink, then take a quart of cream, put in as much sugar as will make it sweet, rub your sugar upon the rind of a lemon to fetch out the essence, put your cream into a pot, mill it to a strong froth, lay as much froth upon a sieve as will fill the dish you intend to put your trifle in, put the remainder of your cream into a tossing pan, with a stick of cinnamon, the yolks of four eggs, well beat, and sugar to your taste, set them over a gentle fire, stir it one way till it is thick, then take it off the fire, pour it upon your maccaroons, when it is cold put on your frothed cream, lay round it different coloured sweetmeats, and small shot comfits in, and figures or flowers.

Another trifle of the late eighteenth century comes from the little known north-country writer Sarah Mason in her *The New Experienced English House-keeper* (c. 1790). We like her reference to laying the froth on 'a tiffany', for which see the Glossary.

To make a Trifle

TAKE macaroons, or round Savoy biscuits, put them into the bottom of a dish, season with a little grated nutmeg, and as much white wine as will cover them, then lay round them a few different sorts of sweet-meats, make a boiled custard, when cold, pour it over them about two inches thick, then heap it up neatly with frothed cream; if in a long dish it is proper for a corner, if round, as a middle dish. To froth the cream, take a pint of the thickest cream you can get, grate the rind of a lemon, and fine sugar, mix all together with the whites of two eggs, wisk them half an hour, before you skim

it, lay the froth on a tiffany to drain, lay it on your trifle just
before you send it up.

Generally, trifle recipes from northern parts are often of special
interest. This certainly applies to the recipe which Fuchsia Dunlop
has sent us, from the 1786 edition of *Mrs Maciver's Cookery and Pastry*.
As will be seen from the text of the recipe, below, it is different from
any of the other earlier ones which we have found. (Mrs Maciver
ran a cookery school in Edinburgh with her colleague Mrs Frazer,
who continued to run it after Mrs Maciver's death in about 1790.
Since the ladies were close colleagues, it is interesting to see that
the trifle recipe which Mrs Frazer published in 1795, and with which
this chapter closes, is of a different sort altogether.)

A Trifle.

Take some white wine and sugar, dip some sugar-biscuit in
it; lay the biscuit in the bottom of a dish, and bring it by
degrees to be high in the middle: when the biscuit is a little
softened with the wine, pour some thick sweet cream over
it; let is stand until the bread has suck'd up the wine and
the cream: if there is any of the liquor left, pour it off. If
you have apples, roast some of them, and order them in the
same way as in the last receipt; lay a covering of apples on
the biscuit; then cover it all over with whipt cream, and drop
some currant-jelly on it.

We close this chapter with another recipe from Scotland, referred
to above, which Ivan Day kindly sent us. This is from Mrs Frazer's
The Practice of Cookery, Pastry, Confectionary, Pickling, Preserving ... ,
1795. He says that he has made this a number of times, once with
the suggestion of preserved gooseberries around the base, which
look very attractive. Note that by 'the shape of a small sugar loaf'
is meant something like a pyramid, which looks very impressive.
For her use of myrtle, see the Glossary.

A trifle.

Make a spunge cake agreeable to the receipt p. 185 [see below], cut it in thin slices, and dip it in some white wine and sugar mixed. Then cover the bottom of a plate with some of the slices, and spread over them preserved rasps, strawberries or sliced apples. Then put on lairs of cake and fruit till you get the trifle into the shape of a small sugar loaf. Then stick a sprig of myrtle into the top of it.

Then take a choppin [two and a quarter litres] of cream, half a mutchkin [200 ml] of wine, three ounces of sugar, the paring of a lemon, and a stick of cinnamon; whisk it up to a strong snow, and as it rises, lift it up and drain it on the back of a sieve; after it has stood an hour, lay it all over the trifle, and heap it as high upon the head of it as you can.

Garnish the trifle all over with currant cream, angelica, and whole red currants, stick in a bunch of them in the myrtle. You may also lay green and preserved gooseberries around the borders of the plate it is served upon.

Mrs Frazer's separate recipe for Red Currant Cream, one of her suggested garnishes, is charming and reads as follows:

Cast the white of an egg to a snow, and add to it two table spoonfuls of red currant jelly; but take care that there are no rasps in it, as they prevent the cream from rising; then take a small whisk, and whisk it close one way, till it is of a fine pale pink colour, and so thick that it will not drop from the whisk. — This is a beautiful garnish for all milk and cream dishes.

It remains to add that Mrs Frazer's sponge cake is made with 12 eggs, 1 lb sugar and a half pound of flour. It is seasoned with 'the grate of three or four lemons'.

CHAPTER THREE

TRIFLES IN NINETEENTH-CENTURY BRITAIN

The nineteenth century, as one would expect, abounds in trifle recipes, often with very imposing titles – 'An Excellent', 'An Elegant', 'A Grand', 'Queen of Trifles'.

Mrs Rundell, calling herself 'A Lady', was responsible for the cookery book which was most popular during the first half of the century. This was *A New System of Domestic Cookery*, first published in 1806, followed by numerous other editions later on.

When her book originally came out the trifling content was clear and unsurprising. She had recipes for An Excellent Trifle, Gooseberry or Apple Trifle and Chantilly Cake or Cake Trifle. The first of these is given below. It is a good, clear recipe, with no real surprises.

An excellent Trifle.

Lay macaroons and ratafia-drops over the bottom of your dish, and pour in as much raisin-wine as they will suck up; which when they have done, pour on them cold rich custard made with more eggs than directed in the foregoing pages, and some rice-flour. It must stand two or three inches thick – on that put a layer of raspberry jam, and cover the whole with a very high whip made the day before, of rich cream, the whites of two well beaten eggs, sugar, lemon peel and raisin wine, well beat with a whisk kept only to whip syllabubs and creams. If made the day before used, it has quite a different taste, and is solid and far better.

The trifling problems which emerge from Mrs Rundell's book all seem to start when the book was already more than thirty years old. One is the matter of Indian Trifle, and the other has to do with her use of rice cakes. We examine each in turn.

In an edition of 1842 we find what we think is the first recipe for an 'Indian Trifle', a slightly mysterious confection which survived in the literature for some decades (Mrs Beeton, for example, gave a recipe in 1861) but then faded from sight. It reminded us somewhat of the Indian *firni*. This is a sweet milky dessert, to be eaten cold, made either with cornflour or rice flour or both, usually flavoured with rosewater and/or cardamom and decorated with chopped or ground almonds or pistachios. It is perfectly possible that in the Anglo-Indian culture of the period British people would have seen a resemblance between the traditional English trifle which could not easily be taught to their Indian cooks and *firni*, which the cooks were completely accustomed to preparing. Hence, perhaps, the hybrid name. Whatever the explanation is, here is the recipe which someone inserted in Mrs Rundell's book.

An Indian Trifle.

Boil a quart of new milk with a large piece of cinnamon; thicken it with flour of rice, first wetted with cold milk; and sweeten to your taste. Pour it into a dish; and when cold cut it into the shape of a star, or any other shape you please. Take out the spare rice, and fill the intervals with boiled custard. Ornament with slit almonds and spots of currant-jelly.

[NOTE. Mrs Beeton's version gives quantities which may be helpful. They are as follows: 1 quart of milk, the rind of ½ large lemon, sugar to taste, 5 heaped tablespoons of rice-flour, 1 oz of sweet almonds, and half a pint of custard. Mini-warning (from Helen): *firni* is notorious for 'catching' on the bottom of the pan. Be on guard against this. And I hope you have better luck than I did – my rice-flour mixture would not set properly!]

RICE CAKES

The use of rice flour in the preceding recipe leads naturally to a discussion of 'rice cakes' as an ingredient for trifles. Rice cakes in

English cookery books go back at least as far as Mrs Raffald (1773) and appeared regularly through the nineteenth century, reaching a kind of zenith in the monumental work by Garrett (c. 1895) where there are altogether 16 recipes for rice cakes. However, their use in trifles is relatively rare. Indeed, the only examples we have found are Mrs Rundell's eccentric Cake Trifle and the interesting recipe from Meg Dods given later in this chapter.

First, the Cake Trifle, with its alternative title, and including its Rice Cake recipe:

Chantilly Cake, or Cake Trifle.

Bake a rice-cake in a mould [as directed below]. When cold, cut it round about two inches from the edge with a sharp knife, taking care not to perforate the bottom. Put in a thick custard, and some tea-spoonfuls of raspberry-jam, and then put on a high whip.

Rice Cake.

Mix ten ounces of ground rice, three ounces of flour, eight ounces of pounded sugar; then sift by degrees into eight yolks and six whites of eggs, and the peel of a lemon shread so fine that it is quite mashed; mix the whole well in a tin stewpan over a very slow fire with a whisk, then put it immediately into the oven in the same, and bake forty minutes.

The next item in our survey comes from a large volume called the *Family Receipt Book*, published around 1810. It is by far the most imposing of the recipes we have considered so far.

A Grand Trifle.

The trifle being generally considered as an article to be prepared with the utmost delicacy of taste as well as of appearance is judged worthy of particular attention. The glass in which it is served up should be beautifully formed as well as cut, and sufficiently large and elevated to convey an idea of grandeur – At the bottom of this elegant depository of light and airy delicacies, put a layer of fine spunge Savoy biscuits; over them, another of ratafias; and a third, of macaroons: strewing, between each two layers, and on the top of the last, a mixture of blanched and pounded almonds; with candied citron, orange peel, and pine-apple chips, cut small and a little finely beaten mace and nutmeg. Pour half a pint or more of sherry, Lisbon, or fine old mountain wine, over the cakes, according to the quantity which they may be found capable of imbibing; and, in the mean time, prepare a custard to cover them, in the following manner – Boil a quart of milk and cream, in equal quantities, with a little lemon peel, some cinnamon, three leaves of laurel [see Glossary], and two or three ounces of sugar, for about twenty minutes; and, while it cools, beat well the yolks of six or eight eggs, and two spoonfuls of rice flour. Then, gradually mixing the milk, a little at a time, well stirring it all the while, and afterward straining it into a stew pan through a hair sieve; place it over the fire, and continue stirring till it comes to a boil, when it must instantly be taken off, and be set to cool. On it's getting about half cold, add half a gill of French brandy; with the same quantity of noyeau, ratafia, or other delicate liqueur. The custard being thus made, and cold is to be put on the cakes; and, over that, some apricot and rasp-berry jam, with a little currant jelly. Then, as a grand covering for the whole, whisk to perfect froth a pint of cream, with the white of an egg, a couple of lumps of sugar rubbed on a lemon or Seville orange, and a glass or two of white wine; skimming off the froth, from time to time, with a pierced spoon, and depositing it at the top of an inverted sieve placed on a dish, to preserve the drainings, that they may be returned and whipped up. When the whole is thoroughly whipped, heap it as high as possible over the custard, &c. and, to crown the whole, sprinkle or garnish the top plenti-fully with those minute coloured comfits, called harlequin seeds or nonpareils. This, it is presumed, will not fail to be considered as a grand trifle. It is easy, by retrenching, more or less, these articles, to form a very good trifle, on this plan adapted to all tastes, circumstances, and occasions.

Meg Dods' Cookery (1826 and later editions – we have used the fifteenth edition of 1883) is the most diverting of Scottish cookery books – a smile on every page (and there are a lot of pages). The real author of the book (Meg Dods was a *nom de plume*) seems to have been keen on trifles. In addition to her 'Elegant Trifle' below, she offers a tipsy cake; a gooseberry or apple trifle (more like a fool); and also a related item called 'Wassail bowl', for which see 'Trifling Relations', page 101.

> *An elegant Trifle.–* Whisk, early in the morning, or the day before you make the *Trifle*, a quart of good cream, with six ounces of sifted sugar, a glass of white wine, the juice and fine grate of a lemon, and a few bits of cinnamon. Take off the froth as it rises, with a sugar-skimmer or silver fish-trowel, and place it to drain on a sieve reversed over a bowl. Whisk till you have enough of the whip, allowing for what it will sink. Next day place in a trifle-dish six fresh-baked sponge-biscuits sliced, or rice trifle-cake [see page 31], or remnants of any good light cake cut down; a dozen ratafia drop-biscuits, and some sweet almonds blanched and split. Pour over them enough of white wine, or ginger-wine, to moisten them completely; next strew a seasoning of grated lemon-peel, and add a thin layer of raspberry or strawberry jam. Have ready a rich and rather thick custard, and pour it over this to the thickness of two inches. Heap the whip above this lightly and gracefully, and garnish with a few light sprigs of flowers of fine colour, or a few bits of very clear currant-jelly laid into the snow-white whip, or a sprinkling of Harlequin comfits. This last is considered antique, but it is still in use.

At this point a roll of drums and a flourish of trumpets are required for we come to the great work of Eliza Acton, who has been justly described as the finest cookery writer in the English language.

This book, *Modern Cookery for Private Families*, which came out in 1845, gives a really good range of trifles – beautifully written recipes

– which include two items with an interesting pair of alternatives. One is tipsy cake, or brandy trifle and the other is Swiss cream, or trifle – see the chapter on 'Trifling Relations'. She also gives a recipe for what she calls 'An Excellent Trifle', linked with one for Syllabubs. So we give both here.

An Excellent Trifle.

Take equal parts of wine and brandy, about a wineglassful of each, or two-thirds of good sherry or Madeira, and one of spirit, and soak in the mixture four sponge-biscuits, and half a pound of macaroons and ratifias; cover the bottom of the trifle-dish with part of these, and pour upon them a full pint of rich boiled custard made with three-quarters of a pint, or rather more, of milk and cream taken in equal portions, and six eggs; and sweetened, flavoured and thickened by the receipt of page 481 [not reproduced here]; lay the remainder of the soaked cakes upon it, and pile over the whole, to the depth of two or three inches, the whipped syllabub of page 476 [see the recipe below], previously well drained; then sweeten and flavour slightly with wine only, less than half a pint of thin cream (or of cream and milk mixed); wash and wipe the whisk, and whip it to the lightest possible froth; take it off with a skimmer and heap it gently over the trifle.

Macaroons and ratifias, ½ lb.; wine and brandy mixed, ½ pint; rich boiled custard, 1 pint; whipped syllabub; light froth to cover the whole, short ½ pint of cream and milk mixed; sugar, dessertspoonful; wine, ½ glassful.

Very superior whipped syllabubs.

Weigh seven ounces of fine sugar and rasp on it the rinds of two fresh sound lemons of good size, then pound or roll it to powder, and put it into a bowl with the strained juice of the lemons, two large glasses of sherry, and two of brandy; when the sugar is dissolved add a pint of very fresh cream, and whisk or mill the mixture well; take off the froth as it rises, and put it into glasses. These syllabubs will remain good for several days, and should always be made if possible, four-and-twenty hours before they are wanted for table. The full flavour of the lemon-rind is obtained with less trouble than in rasping, by paring it very thin indeed, and infusing it for some hours in the juice of the fruit.

Sugar, 7 oz ; rind and juice of lemons, 2 ; sherry, 2 large wineglassesful ; brandy, 2 wineglassesful ; cream, 1 pint.

Obs.– These proportions are sufficient for two dozens or more of syllabubs: they are often made with almost equal quantities of wine and cream, but are considered less wholesome without a portion of brandy.

In the nineteenth century, manuscripts are a rich source for trifle recipes and the recipe for 'Steeped cake, or Trifle' below comes from a nineteenth-century manuscript recipe in York Archives and can be attributed – so food historian Laura Mason of York tells us – with reasonable confidence to the wife of a Canon of York Minster.

A Steeped Cake, or Trifle

An excellent side dish, 2d course – Cut a lemon cake smooth on all sides, put it in a deep dish & by degrees pour upon it as much wine as will completely moisten it – then place it upon the dish, on which you intend to send it to Table. – Cover it over with raspberry jam – pour a rich Custard round it – stick blanched almonds upon the preserve, & then surround the Cake with frothed cream.

An engaging book called *Cre-Fydd's Family Fare: The Young Housewife's Daily Assistant* (1866) offers something rather different: a fruit trifle with a base below the fruit and a very high alcohol content.

Gooseberry Trifle

Cut up six ounces of sponge-cake into slices half an inch thick; lay it on the bottom of a glass dish that will hold three pints. Mix together a wineglassful and a half of brandy, half a wineglassful of whiskey, half a wineglassful of gin, and a tablespoonful of sifted loaf sugar; pour this equally over the cake, and let it soak while the following preparations are made. Pick, wash, and wipe dry a quart of fine green goose-berries; put them into a brass skillet, with three-quarters of a pound of loaf sugar, and simmer over a very slow fire till they are quite tender but not broken; turn them into a basin to get cold. Boil a quarter of a pound of loaf sugar and the thin peel of half a lemon in a pint of new milk; moisten two tablespoonsful of Oswego flour [see Glossary], with half a gill of cold milk; add four well-beaten fresh eggs; beat for five minutes; then stir in the milk while hot, but not boiling; pour the mixture into the skillet, and stir over a very slow fire till it begins to thicken; then pour it into a basin. Take out the peel; stir frequently, and when nearly cold add thirty drops of the essence of vanilla; lay the gooseberries on the cake, smooth the surface and pour over the cream; let it stand in a cool place three hours before serving.

In the 1890s Theodore Francis Garrett edited an enormous collection of recipes (so huge that it is usually found in eight large volumes), and it is in this vast repository that we find the largest group of trifle recipes published up to that point – no fewer than sixteen. Garrett probably held the record until the book by May Byron in 1923 (see page 40) which contained eighteen. And that record, we think stood until 2001, when the present work was published, with its more than 90 recipes for trifles and trifling relations.

Garrett makes no secret of his partiality for trifles, introducing his long entry on the subject as follows:

> **TRIFLES**. – These are exceptionally English dishes, and are held in very poor esteem by the foreign pastry-cook, who probably attaches some greater importance to the name than is necessary. Webster connects the word with the French *truffe* or *truffle*, signifying anything of little note or importance. From the following receipts it will be seen that these Trifles are not by any means unimportant as dishes.

His recipes include Moulded Swiss Trifle, Old-fashioned Trifle and Tipsy Trifle. In addition he gives two savoury ones (for one of them see p. iii). The crowning glory of his collection is perhaps the recipe which follows, with its regal title.

Queen of Trifles.– Lay ½ lb of lady fingers or square sponge cakes at the bottom of a trifle-dish; pour over them, a spoonful at a time, 1 glass of brandy, lay over them, a thin layer of fruit jelly or jam, strew over this ½ lb of crystallized fruit chopped fine, on top of this put a layer of macaroons (about ½ lb), moisten them with 1 glass of sherry, and cover them with a thick layer of jam or sweet fruit jelly. Set the dish in a cool place, and let the wine and brandy soak into the cakes. Blanch ½ lb of sweet almonds, put them into a mortar, and pound them to a paste, adding a little rose-water to prevent their oiling. Scald 1 pint of milk, and when very hot put the almond paste into it. Keep stirring it for one minute, and then stir in the yolks of four eggs, well beaten, with ¼ lb of powdered white sugar. Keep on stirring for three minutes longer, and then add 1 tablespoonful of cornflour blended with a little cold milk. Still continue stirring till the custard has thickened well, and then take it from the fire and beat it for awhile, or else pour it backwards and forwards from one jug to another several times, to prevent lumps from forming as it cools. Sweeten 1 pint of rich cream to taste with powdered white sugar and whisk it to a stiff froth. When the custard is quite cold, pour it over the soaked macaroons, &., in the trifle dish, and pile high over it the whipped cream.

Garrett's book, entitled *The Encyclopaedia of Practical Cookery*, appeared around 1895. The 1890s were a good decade for cookery books, because they also saw publication, in 1898, of *A Practical Cookery Book* by Mrs Roundell, an author who is much less well known than she deserves to be. Her 'family recipe' for a trifle makes charming reading and can be relied on to produce a charming result. Don't forget your long-handled spoon; and do heed her advice, if you conveniently can, that a trifle is best made a day in advance.

Trifle.– (Family Recipe.) – Trifle should be made the day before it is wanted, and should be served in a china bowl. Lay six sponge biscuits close together at the bottom of the bowl, and pour over them as much sherry as they will absorb. Then put a layer of ratafia cakes or fresh macaroons (those from a tin are much too hard), and sprinkle them with a little sherry. Put another layer of stale sponge cake, and spread it with strawberry or raspberry jam.

Make a custard of half a pint of cream boiled for ten minutes with the very finely pared rind of one lemon; add another half pint of cream, and boil it ten minutes more. Strain the cream into a basin, sweeten it a little, and let it get cold. When it is cold, beat the yolks of six eggs for a quarter of an hour, strain them with the cream into a pan over a low fire, and stir with a plated spoon till it thickens. Put the custard to cool.

Whip a pint of cream, sweeten it with a little sugar which has been rubbed on a lemon, and add to it one tablespoonful of brandy. As the froth rises take it off in a spoon, lay it on a dish, and leave it to become a little firm.

Shake pounded ratafias over the top of the Trifle, pour the custard upon them, and finally pile up the froth of cream as high as possible. In helping Trifle use a long-handled spoon, and go down to the bottom. Tipsy Cake is Trifle under another name, with the addition that the sponge cakes are stuck with almonds, and that a little red currant jelly is laid on the custard.

CHAPTER FOUR

BRITISH TRIFLES IN THE FIRST HALF OF THE TWENTIETH CENTURY

The style of trifle recipes changed noticeably in this period, anyway from 1914 onwards. No doubt the two world wars and the Depression which occurred between them conspired to produce a rather more frugal and terse kind of recipe, in this as in other branches of cookery. Moreover, the first half of the twentieth century did not see the emergence of great cookery writers such as Eliza Acton, but instead seemed to produce (with of course some exceptions like *The Gentle Art of Cookery* by Mrs Leyel and Olga Hartley, 1925) works of a more pedestrian nature.

Naturally, at the beginning of the century, in the Edwardian era, writers were still influenced by the nineteenth-century tradition of elaborate and elegant dishes. Indeed the first recipe in this chapter, which comes from *A La Mode Cookery* by Mrs de Salis, 1902, has a title which explicitly refers back to the previous century. It is complex and rich (and quite alcoholic!), with interesting features such as the use of greengage jam and ginger wine. (Oddly, what is clearly the same recipe occurs in Elizabeth Craig's *Court Favourites*, 1953, where it is called Old-Fashioned Tipsy Kent Squire and is simply attributed to the mid-nineteenth century.)

TRIFLE À LA OLD CENTURY

This must be prepared nine or ten hours before it is required. Take a pound sponge-cake rather stale, a quarter of a pound of each of greengage, apricot and strawberry jam, a quarter of a pound of orange marmalade, half a pint of marsala or raisin wine, a wineglassful of brandy, the same of curaçao and ginger wine, five ounces of loaf sugar, six fresh eggs, one pint of milk, half a pint of thick cream (Devonshire cream preferred), two ounces of blanched sweet almonds, one ounce of ratafias, and a teaspoonful of vanilla essence.

Cut the cake into five slices. Put the top slice aside and spread the other four with the different jams. Put two ounces of sugar into the wine, mix the brandy and liqueurs in also; lay the ratafias in a glass dish, and on them the bottom slice of the cake. Pour a little of the wine over them, put on another slice of cake on the top of the other, and more wine and so on till the cake is built up; keep pouring the wine over till it is all used up.

Make a rich custard flavoured with brandy, let it get quite cold; cut the almonds in pointed slices, stick the top of the cake with them, and when ready to serve pour over the custard.

May Byron was a remarkably prolific author who flourished from 1914 to 1932 and whose comprehensive *Pudding Book* was published in 1923. This book has many interesting features, including an arresting passage on the nature of puddings (reproduced in *The Oxford Companion to Food*, 1999). She makes a point of distinguishing in her 1070 recipes between 'plain' and 'rich', with the emphasis on the former, as befitted the social and economic context in which she was working. However, it is interesting to see that her introductory definition of 'Trifle' ends with an exhortation not to count the cost:

Trifle is difficult to define, though by no means so to devour.

It is a confection covered with whipped cream or whisked white of egg, and its basis is cake or pastry soaked in wine, plus macaroons, fruit, blanched almonds, etc., etc., etc. It is in a sense a trifle "light as air," but in no sense an "unconsidered trifle." It requires elaboration, imagination, and ingenuity to be a complete success, also some recklessness as regards economy.

In a further note she remarks that: 'This tempting dish may ... be varied in many delightful ways; nothing can stale its infinite variety. And it need not necessarily be troublesome or expensive. It is as pleasant to the eye as to the palate, on account of its contour, colour, and texture; and is by no means difficult to make.'

Altogether, May Byron has recipes for eighteen trifles, including items which she presents under the sub-heading 'Various Trifling Preparations'.

It was very hard choosing which of her trifle recipes to give here but we settled on three favourites, and these show particularly well the full glory and diversity of the trifle.

We start with Countess Trifle. Whoever the Countess was, she obviously believed in simplicity, for this trifle has very little adornment; the cake is not soaked in any liqueur or juice and there is no final topping of cream or meringue or decorations. A truly minimalist approach.

Countess Trifle

Cut five sponge cakes in half. Place on a dish with alternate layers of fruit, the last layer being fruit. Make a nice thick custard, and flavour with orange flower water; sweeten to taste, and, when nearly cold pour it over the fruit.

Our second choice from May Byron is an unusual item, being a baked trifle. Since the recipe is quite vague, we have added explanatory notes based on our test. NB, the end result is quite delicious.

Pear Trifle

Have some pears cooked [as indicated in Notes]. Line the bottom of a pudding-dish with slices of sponge cake sprinkled with coconut; then put in the pears, and pour over them three beaten egg yolks which have been whisked with half a cupful of sugar. Place in a moderate oven till brown, then cover with a meringue made of the three egg whites whisked up with half a cupful of sugar. Return to the oven, and let the meringue become coloured; remove, and serve cold.

[NOTES: We recommend sweet and aromatic pears such as Comice. We used three, poached in a syrup (125 ml water,

125 g sugar and the juice of ¼ lemon). We suggest 4 or 5 trifle sponges, sprinkled with 3 tablespoons of desiccated coconut.]

We liked the sound of May Byron's 'Lemon Trifle' (a lemon flavour is always attractive) and give her text below which once again is quite vague as to amounts, so it is followed by our interpretation of ingredients.

Lemon Trifle

Pile in the centre of a glass dish a sufficiency of sponge fingers, soft biscuits, and macaroons. Moisten these with a little light wine. Prepare a lemon cream mixture with half a pint of water, four ounces of lump sugar, the grated rind of a fresh lemon and a little of the juice, the yolks of two eggs, an ounce of fresh butter, and a dessertspoonful of cornflour moistened with lemon juice. Bring to boiling point and pour it over the cakes. When cold, cover with a meringue made from the whites of the eggs, sugar, and cream stiffly whipped.

[Notes: We supplied missing quantities as follows: 8 boudoir biscuits; 8 macaroons; 16 tbs white wine (medium sweet); and for the meringue 110 g caster sugar and 140 ml double cream.]

Violet Farebrother, who was then well known in theatrical circles, contibuted this interesting recipe to *The Stage Favourites Cook Book* (1923). Elizabeth Craig, the gifted cookery writer who edited this anthology, evidently thought well of the recipe for she reproduced it long afterwards in her own book *Hotch Potch* (1978). We like it too.

AN EASTER TRIFLE

1 small tin pineapple; 6 small sponge cakes; apricot jam; raspberry jam; ½ pint rich custard; ¾ pint whipping cream; castor sugar; vanilla essence; crystallized rose leaves [petals?]; crystallized violets.

Cut a small tin of pine-apple slices into small pieces and arrange in the bottom of a crystal dish. Then cut 6 small sponge cakes in half lengthwise, and spread 3 with apricot and 3 with raspberry jam. Put the pieces together again, then quarter them crosswise and spread one side of each quarter with jam, using the apricot for the raspberried ones and the raspberry for the apricot. Pile up the cakes on top of the pine-apple, then slowly pour over the pine-apple syrup from the tin, just enough to soak the cake. Leave for 20 minutes, then cover with ½ pint rich custard. When cold, whip ¾ pint of cream, sweeten to taste with castor sugar and flavour with a little vanilla essence. Pile up rockily on top and decorate with crystallized rose leaves and violets.

Angostura Bitters, originated by Dr Siegart in Guayana in 1824, is world famous for its use in drinks. Less well known are its uses in puddings and sweet dishes. The rare booklet *For Home Use*, published at Port-of-Spain in Trinidad in the 1930s has a collection of such recipes, including "Angostura" Trifle, as follows:

"ANGOSTURA" TRIFLE

Slice 6 stale sponge cakes in halves, putting raspberry jam between top and bottom. Arrange compactly in a fairly wide glass dish. Next put a ½ teaspoonful of "Angostura" in a wineglassful of sherry, mix and pour evenly over the sponge cakes. Arrange on top a neat mound of ratafias or macaroons and cover with a cupful of custard. Thoroughly whip ½ pint of cream and lay it gently on the contents of the dish and decorate with angelica, cherries and shredded almonds. Prepare not less than 2 hours before serving.

In 1925 Mrs Leyel and her literary partner Olga Hartley produced a romantic cookery book, *The Gentle Art of Cookery*, which had a great influence. Mrs Leyel subsequently produced a series of small books on subjects such as *Picnics for Motorists*, and – the source we use here – *Puddings*.

The writer's Special Trifle

For this and for all trifles gooseberry jam is to be preferred, and failing this raspberry, plum and black currant jam should be substituted.

12 sponge cakes, 6 ozs. jam, ¾ pint milk, ¼ pint cream, 2 eggs, rum or sherry, vanilla, crystallized cherries.

Shred the sponge cakes into a flat silver dish and soften them with a little milk to which three or four tablespoons of rum or sherry have been added. Then prepare a custard by boiling the milk with a vanilla pod and sugar to taste and pouring it (after the pod has been removed) over the well beaten eggs. The custard can be finished in a jug placed in a saucepan of boiling water.

Pour the custard over the sponge cakes, and when cold whip the cream and rake it over the top of the custard, taking care not to disturb the custard itself. Decorate with a few crystallized cherries, but if the custard is not firm enough to take them use split almonds, hundreds and thousands, or trifle leaves.

[NOTES: For trifle leaves, see the Glossary. The jam is to be spooned on to the shredded sponge cakes.]

Now comes a 1930s Leicestershire recipe which we have adapted from 'Mrs Toone's Apple Snow Trifle' in *English Puddings – Sweet and Savoury* (1981) by Mary Norwak.

We like this recipe because it gives us an opportunity to introduce readers to another variation of topping – a light and frothy apple snow – which replaces the usual cream or syllabub.

Use an apple variety which becomes light and fluffy when cooked. We used Ellison's Orange, a 1950s variety from Alan and Jane Davidson's Chelsea garden.

APPLE SNOW TRIFLE
(to serve four)

450 g apples; 65 g caster sugar; strip of lemon peel; 300 ml whole milk; 1 vanilla pod; 2 eggs; 4 trifle spongecakes; 4 tbs amaretto liqueur or sherry; blackberry jam or bramble jelly; toasted flaked almonds.

Peel and core the apples and cut them into slices. Put into a saucepan with 50 g sugar, lemon peel and 2 tbsp water. Simmer until the apples are soft.

Remove the lemon peel and purée the apples in a blender or rub them through a sieve. Allow to cool.

Heat the milk with the vanilla pod just to boiling point. Remove the vanilla pod (washing and drying it for future use). Separate the eggs and stir the egg yolks with the remaining sugar. Pour on the hot milk, whisk well and return the pan to the heat. Continue stirring over a low heat until the custard becomes thick and creamy. Remove from the heat and allow to cool a little.

Split the spongecakes in half through the centres and sandwich back together with the blackberry jam or bramble jelly. Arrange on the base of a glass dish. Sprinkle with the amaretto liqueur or sherry.

Pour the custard over the spongecakes. Leave until cold.

Whisk the egg whites to stiff peaks and fold them into the apple purée. Pile the apple foam on top of the custard and decorate with toasted flaked almonds or according to fancy.

We have a small booklet entitled *More ... Favourite Puddings of Rural England*, compiled by the Editor of *Favourite Puddings of Rural*

England. It is a little gem, full of interesting recipes arranged in alphabetical order. Its price was only threepence.

The trifles which the compilers offered included the following recipe which falls in the quick and easy category and does not involve making a custard.

After selecting the recipe, we found that it echoes one offered by Garrett (for whom see page 36), who classified his more up-market version under Ratafia rather than Trifle and put '(American)' after the title. So the recipe for the Rural England people was quick and easy in another sense – all they had to do was lift it from Garrett and change some of his ingredients to make it easier for trifle-makers in rural areas (e.g. the liqueur Noyau is changed to almond essence). Still, they did make changes, all in the direction of simplicity, so credit for the recipe stays with them.

Ratafia Trifle

Cut up one tinned pineapple. Put in a glass dish, and sprinkle with two ounces of castor sugar. Cover with four ounces of ratafias, and pour over two glasses of sherry or home-made wine. When well soaked pile on the top one pint of whipped cream, sweetened and flavoured with almond essence. Decorate with crystallized fruits.

Recipe books produced during the Second World War often concentrate on the economies and substitutions which were necessary during and for some time after that period. One of the best, in our view, is *Anthology of Puddings* by Irene Veal (1942). She rose above the temporary difficulties, boldly including some recipes which could only be made after peace had returned and cajoling many famous people and institutions to contribute recipes. Almost two pages are devoted to the Savoy Hotel recipe for Woolton Pie, perhaps the most famous of the dishes created to be compatible with war-time conditions. Although this is not really anything to do with trifles, we must take the opportunity to remark that Irene Veal shows in detail how the official Ministry of Food recipe for this pie differed from that of the Savoy, where it was invented. She was backing a winner here, since fifty years later the pie was given a new lease of life when Professor Nicholas Kurti addressed The Royal Society on the subject and gave this august company helpings of the pie.

We pause here to note that some lighter notes are struck by the inclusion, for example, of what is described as an exceedingly indigestible item, 'Big-hearted Tart (or you silly little flan)' from the comedian Arthur Askey and a recipe in verse for Teacup Pudding, the last lines of which served as a vehicle for A.A. Thomson's views on contemporary music:

> So give it to your husband, ma'am,
> The perfect way to coax him,
> But give it to a crooner and
> I hope the pudding chokes him.

Having by means of this lengthly preamble established the credentials of Irene Veal as a writer who was both thoughtful and entertaining, we proceed to the trifle which she commended to her readers. The recipe came from Reginald Foort, the BBC organist whose sonorous music penetrated every home in Britain. It is laid out below as it was presented in Irene Veal's book.

REGINALD FOORT
has large ideas, and sends the following recipe for a
TRIFLE
which proves this assertion.

He writes as follows: "My favourite pudding is a trifle. I can't give you the technical details in the style of Mrs. Beeton, but: Take a lot of not-too-stale sponge cakes; split in half longwise, add a lot of jam – preferably strawberry – and make them into a jam sandwich. Place in a deep glass dish and more or less soak with sherry. Then pour over lots of custard, allow to set, pour lots of whipped cream over, and decorate the top with lots of white skinned almonds and some cherries. Stick in the refrigerator to cool until served."

Mrs Kirk's *Tried Favourites* has appeared in (almost) countless editions since it was first published at Selkirk in 1900 'to reduce the heavy debt on our church'. The title page bore the down-to-earth exclamation: 'Oh, bother your books, and all their receipting; the proof of the pudding is in the eating.'

Our copy of this perennial best seller is the 'Twenty-sixth and Enlarged Edition – Seven hundred and thirty-second thousand' (1948). In this version it had a number of trifle recipes, including Apple, Chocolate, German (with a rice pudding base) and Lemon as well as what she calls 'Trifle (1)' and 'Trifle (2)'. Of these we give the last, which is interesting because the layers are formed in a different way and the strawberry jam has ground almonds sprinkled over it.

TRIFLE (2)

Put a good layer of strawberry jam at bottom of crystal dish. Squeeze a little lemon juice over, which gives a freshness to strawberries. Sprinkle some ground almonds over, then some sponge cakes, sliced and pierced with sharp-pointed knife. Pour over 3 or 4 tablespoons milk, then ½ pint boiled custard, after letting milk settle, then ½ pint whipped cream, flavoured same as custard.

CHAPTER FIVE

BRITISH TRIFLES FROM 1950 ONWARDS

Patterns of many things changed during these fifty years, and the pace of change was increasing towards the end of the century. There was much more foreign travel, often opening eyes to new ways of doing things and new ingredients. The whole industry of teaching cookery, previously more or less confined to catering colleges and kindred institutions, burgeoned to an extraordinary effect, perhaps mainly because of the influence of television. There was also a qualitative change in writing about food and cookery, symbolized for many people by the work of Elizabeth David, with her protegée Jane Grigson following in her footsteps.

It is not surprising that effects of these seismic changes had reached into the peaceful backwaters where people were making trifles for birthday parties and other celebrations. However, if one considers its wide popularity, it is surprising to see that the trifle does not loom very large in the writings of leading British cookery writers of the period we are considering. To be sure, recipes for it may be found without difficulty, but one has the general impression that it was viewed as a somewhat 'common' confection and that it was seen during this period as a cheapened and distorted version of whatever had been the original 'pure' trifle.

Elizabeth David (writing in the 1960s – see page 246 of *An Omelette and a Glass of Wine*, 1984) is eloquent and witty on the subject. Noting that syllabub and trifle co-existed for a century or so, she lamented the fact that eventually 'the trifle came to reign in the syllabub's stead', and applauded signs that in some circles the syllabub was now making a comeback. In characteristically partisan vein, she continues:

> ... and before long the party pudding of the English was not any more the fragile whip of cream contained in a little

glass, concealing within its innocent white froth a powerful alcoholic punch, but a built-up confection of sponge fingers and ratafias soaked in wine and brandy, spread with jam, clothed in an egg-and-cream custard, topped with a syllabub and strewen with little coloured comfits. Came 1846, the year that Alfred Bird brought forth custard powder; and Mr Bird's brain-child grew and grew until all the land was covered with custard made with custard powder and the Trifle had become custard's favourite resting-place. The wine and lemon-flavoured cream whip or syllabub which had crowned the Trifle had begun to disappear. Sponge cake left over from millions of nursery teas usurped the place of sponge fingers and the little bitter almond macaroons called ratafias. Kitchen sherry replaced Rhenish and Madeira and Lisbon wines. Brandy was banished. The little coloured comfits – sugar coated coriander seeds and caraways – bright as tiny tiddlywinks, went into a decline and in their stead reigned candied angelica and nicely varnished glacé cherries.

However, in an essay entitled 'Exigez Le Veritable Cheddar Français' (*Wine and Food*, No. 122, summer 1964 and reprinted in *An Omelette and a Glass of Wine*, 1984) Elizabeth David exhibited a protective attitude to trifles. Having referred with qualified approval to newly-invented cheese dishes (including French Welsh Rabbit) recommended by the publicity agents of Guinness and of the Trappist monks who own the Port-du-Salut cheese factory in north-western France, she continued:

Recipes disseminated by such bodies – one does appreciate that in the case of the Trappists a spokesman is essential – are bound to be suspect, but not all the public relations cookery experts are as cruelly anti-humanitarian as the lady who publicized the traditional Welsh trifle for St. David's Day to be made with one tin of fruit salad and one packet of Birds Pineapple Instant Whip, a leek confected from angelica, piped cream, cocoa powder and desiccated coconut adding the finishing festive touches.

The career of Marguerite Patten as a cookery writer began in the shadow of the Second World War and has extended already into the new millennium. It thus covers, rather precisely, the last half of the twentieth century, and her writings constitute a kind of touchstone against which to measure what others were writing and also to what extent things were changing. She has been a truly representative writer, eschewing fancy fashions and always in tune with the practices and aspirations of the majority of the population.

So, it is appropriate that the first recipe in this chapter should come from one of her earliest books, *Learning to Cook with Marguerite Patten* (1955). She provides instructions for a basic trifle, the first of the two reproduced below, but also for a Richer Trifle (using sherry instead of fruit juice and with whipped cream and a more elaborate decoration); a Fruit Trifle (add the fruit as well as the fruit syrup and again use whipped cream); and the Jelly Trifle which is the second recipe to appear below.

Trifle

3 sponge cakes, 1 good tablespoon jam, preferably raspberry. 1 tablespoon blanched almonds. About ½ teacup fruit syrup, from a tin of fruit or from stewed fruit. 1 pint custard sauce, made according to directions on packet.

Split the sponge cakes into two or three layers and spread with jam. Put into a glass dish, and pour the fruit syrup over it, allowing it to soak into the sponge cakes. Pour the hot custard over. Put a plate on top to prevent a skin forming, and when cold decorate with the almonds.

Jelly Trifle. Make a pint of fruit-flavoured jelly. Soak the sponge cakes in a small quantity of fruit syrup, rather under ½ teacup, otherwise the jelly will not set. Pour over half the hot jelly, together with fruit, if wished. Allow jelly to set, then pour cold custard over it. It must be cold, otherwise it will make the jelly soft again. When the custard is firm decorate with whipped jelly, cherries, nuts, and cream. To whip the jelly, put into a large bowl and whisk vigorously.

In the following decade Helen Cox, a New Zealander, had occasion to say that there were 'few English desserts more English than the Trifle'. She referred to a great variety of 'off-shoot' recipes which had recently appeared but maintained (correctly) that the genuinely traditional one had so far survived unchanged. In her book *Traditional English Cooking* (1961) she gave this recipe for it. (We have slightly restyled the presentation to make it fit in here.)

ENGLISH TRIFLE

Sponge cake; Raspberry jam; Egg custard; Port wine; Almond macaroons or ratafias; Whipped cream; Vanilla; Castor or icing sugar; Almonds; Cherries

(1) Have enough pieces of sponge cake to fill your crystal dish about half. It would be approximately ¾ lb. The pieces could be about 2 inches by 4 inches. Spread them generously with raspberry jam.

(2) Make an egg custard (*below*).

(3) Pour 4 or 5 tablespoons port wine over the cake. Use more if you like. Allow to soak in for a few minutes, then pour the custard over. Cool.

(4) Cover with a layer of almond macaroons. If they are large ones, break them into small pieces. If possible buy the tiny ratafias.

(5) Whip ½ pint cream until stiff (but not into butter!), adding ½ teaspoon vanilla essence and ½ teaspoon castor or icing sugar. Spread this over the trifle. Stick all over with blanched, sliced almonds, and decorate with a few halved cherries.

EGG CUSTARD: Heat 1 cup milk (½ pint), using either a double boiler or small saucepan. Beat 1 egg or 2 egg yolks with 1 rounded tablespoon sugar. Stir into milk and cook gently until it will just coat the spoon. Do not allow to boil. It is a delicious custard and pours like cream. Flavour with a few drops of vanilla essence.

Alan writes: I must first have tasted trifle in the home of my grand-mother at Bearsden near Glasgow. I have no distinct memory of the occasion, but I like to think that when I make my favourite trifle, a Scottish one from the second edition (1963) of *The Scots Kitchen* by Marian McNeill, I am coming very close to what my grandmother made. Invited by a famous cookery writer to take a dessert to supper she was giving for a score of others, I took this, and found that everyone raved about it.

SCOTS TRIFLE

Stale sponge cakes or rice cake, ratafias, raspberry or strawberry jam, lemon rind, sherry, brandy (optional), rich custard, cream, garnishing.

Split six individual sponge cakes and spread thickly with jam. Put together again and arrange in a shallow glass dish. Pound about eighteen ratafia biscuits and strew over the sponges. Sprinkle with the grated rind of half a lemon. Over this pour a gill of sherry (not too dry) and two tablespoonfuls of brandy, then three-quarters of a pint of rich custard. Allow to stand for at least an hour. Whip half a pint of cream, add sugar to taste and flavour with vanilla or Drambuie. Pile this over the custard and garnish with crystallized rose petals (pink) or cherries and angelica; ratafias and pistachio nuts; pink sugar with a border of ratafias; harlequin comfits; or as desired.

[NOTES: Instead of sherry I used 125 ml of Marsala. For the sponge cakes I noted that rice cakes were a permissible alter-native, but stayed with sponge, using four 'cup sponge cakes', sliced horizontally to make 2 layers at the bottom of the dish; I used 24 ratafia biscuits, but 30 might be better; the grated rind of half a lemon seemed insufficient and I recommend twice the quantity. The custard recipe I used was the one for the *PPC* 50 trifle (page 61). I chose Drambuie as the flavour-ing for the whipped cream, using approximately 2 tsp. For decoration I chose crystallized rose petals in a pattern with a few very thin strips of angelica. Very Bearsden.]

Much more could be said about Scotland. But it is time to pass on to Ireland, which is an equally powerful stronghold of trifles. Every family there has its own treasured recipe, or so Myrtle Allen (1977) implies, in giving her own family favourite, prefaced by these charming observations:

It's a bit annoying when somebody refers to a 'a lady's wine' or 'a man's book'. When it comes to trifle, however, I must admit men, in particular, become passionately interested.

I once heard three men arguing about how to make the one-and-only, authentic trifle. Each man's grandmother had made the trifle of his life, and each made it differently.

One of them had a Drogheda granny who made trifle with sponge cakes spread with raspberry jam, topped with tinned pears and moistened with pear juice. These were covered with a layer of custard and another of cream. No decorations, no sherry.

An East Cork granny, belonging to the second man, dissolved jelly in the juice of tinned peaches or pears and poured this with sherry over sponge cakes. She put the fruit between the layers and topped the lot with whipped cream. She used no custard or decorations.

The third man's rather grand Yorkshire granny put ratafia biscuits, macaroons and sponge cakes in layers in the bowl. She moistened them with sherry, fruit juice and lemon curd. Custard and sometimes cream topped the bowl, and crystallized violets and roses were used for decoration.

My Irish Cook Book by Monica Sheridan (1965) is a pleasantly informal and thoroughly Irish compilation, from which we take her family trifle in its 'party' version.

Visitors' Trifle
(to serve 8)

Our family trifle was usually a hotchpotch of anything that was left over from the day before – stale sponge-cake, the heel end of a jelly, the last of a tin of fruit. The whole thing was smothered in a whiskey-flavoured egg custard and topped with whipped cream.

But that was not considered party fare, which went like this:

1 stale sponge-cake; 4 tablespoons raspberry jam; 1 glass Irish whiskey; 2 glasses sherry; 2 cups egg custard (given below); 2 egg whites; ½ pint cream; 1 tablespoon sugar; 2 oz almonds, blanched and split.

Split the sponge-cake into 4 layers. Spread the layers generously with the jam and restack. Put them in a glass dish. Mix the whiskey and sherry and pour over the layered cake. Cover with a plate and leave to soak for an hour.

For the custard:

1 egg; 2 egg yolks; 1 tablespoon sugar; 2 cups milk.

Beat the egg and egg yolks together with the sugar. Scald the milk and pour over the eggs while beating. Cook the custard over a pan of hot water until it thickens to a cream. Pour it over the cake while hot. Leave to get cold.

Beat the 2 egg whites to a peak. Whip the cream with a half-tablespoon of sugar. Fold the whites into the beaten cream and pile over the trifle. Decorate with the blanched and split almonds, which are spiked into the cream.

The next recipe comes from *Jane Grigson's Fruit Book* (1982). Many people would count this as one of two or three greatest books by a great cookery writer who had a gift for enhancing her recipes by literary allusions and personal reminiscences. Here she tells us that she simply could not leave out her Banana Trifle because, although it has no unusual features apart from the use of banana, it had been 'a particular favourite at Christmas parties for so many years'.

Those who would like to make a trifle which they can attribute to the famous Jane Grigson, but do not fancy banana, will be pleased to hear that the recipe was accompanied by a note saying that in summer one could use cherries, strawberries or raspberries for the bananas, or lightly cooked peach or apricot slices.

It will be seen that Jane Grigson favoured the more traditional topping of syllabub rather than the whipped cream which began to supplant it in the nineteenth century.

Banana Trifle

When you measure out the ingredients, have extra cake or macaroons in reserve. Your large glass bowl may be bigger or squarer than mine, and need odd corners filling in. There is no reason, for instance, why you should not use both maca-roons and cake, or slices of home-made sponge roll with apricot or any other appropriate jam in it. Again, wine can be what you have – we usually bring a small store of Muscat de Frontignan back from France that we save up for Christmas, but other muscat wines can be used instead, or Sauternes.

6 large macaroons or pound of sponge cake slices; kirsch or apricot brandy or fruit eau de vie of an appropriate kind; sweet dessert wine; 500 ml single cream; half a vanilla pod, split; 2 large eggs; 2 large egg yolks; caster sugar from vanilla pod jar; strawberry, raspberry or apricot jam; 2–3 ripe, firm bananas; pared rind and juice of a lemon; 300 ml double cream; pinch nutmeg; toasted almonds and candied peel for decoration.

Make a ground-floor layer of macaroons or cake in the bottom of a large glass bowl. Pour over it 3 tablespoons of whichever spirit you use, and 150 ml wine. Give this a chance to soak in, then add more wine if you think the macaroons or cake are on the dry side.

Make the custard by boiling the single cream with the vanilla pod. Beat eggs and yolks together; pour on the boiling cream, whisking, then return to pan and stir over a low heat until thickened. Sweeten to taste. Cool, remove the vanilla pod.

While the custard cools, spread a layer of jam over the sponge cake or macaroon layer. Then slice the bananas – after peeling them, of course – and arrange the pieces closely together on top.

Spoon the cooled custard carefully over the banana, starting with the outside, then moving in. This prevents the banana slices being dislodged.

At this stage, it is a good idea to leave the trifle in the refrigerator overnight, for everything to bed down together.

At the same time, put the lemon rind and juice in a bowl with 2 tablespoons of whichever spirit you used, and 8 tablespoons of the wine. Next day, strain the juice into a large bowl, and stir in 60 g caster sugar. Still stirring, pour in the cream slowly, and add the nutmeg. Beat with a whisk until the syllabub holds its shape – do not overbeat or the cream will curdle.

Anyone looking for an exquisitely light and frothy dessert for entertaining on those hot lazy days of summer will do well to try this trifle, inspired partly by a *Good Housekeeping* recipe. For information about syllabubs generally, see page 95.

Summer Syllabub Trifle

12–15 boudoir biscuits; 500–750 g mixed summer fruits: raspberries, strawberries (sliced or halved), loganberries, red and black currants; sugar; 16 amaretti biscuits; 3 egg whites; 175 g caster sugar; 150 ml dry white wine; juice of ½ lemon; 2 tbs brandy; 150 ml double cream.

Line a glass bowl with a layer of boudoir biscuits. Cover with the mixed fruits, reserving some of the fruits to decorate the top of the trifle. Sprinkle with a little sugar, according to taste. Top with a layer of amaretti biscuits.

Whisk the egg whites until stiff. Gradually add half the sugar and continue whisking until the meringue holds its shape. Fold in the remaining sugar. Carefully pour the wine, lemon juice and brandy over the egg whites and fold in gently.

Whip the cream until it just holds its shape and then fold this into the frothy meringue mixture. Now pour this over the amaretti. Leave to stand for several hours in a cool place to enable the biscuits to become moist.

Decorate with the reserved fruits.

Our first recipe, loosely based on a Sainsbury's leaflet 'The Taste of Italy', was created by Helen to form part of the nation-wide celebration of Alan's seventy-fourth birthday, and figures in the small and exceedingly rare booklet entitled *Alan Davidson's Tea Time Favourites* (not known to any of the bibliographers) which appeared at that time.

For purists the canned pear halves can be substituted by halves of three fresh pears, poached in a little syrup.

Trifle Belle Hélène

12–15 boudoir biscuits; 3–4 tbs amaretto liqueur; 1 can (410 g) pear halves; 100 g bitter chocolate; 250 g tub of mascarpone; 3 tbs icing sugar, sifted; 100 ml double cream; toasted flaked almonds; angelica.

Arrange the boudoir biscuits in a glass bowl. Sprinkle with the amaretto liqueur and 4 tbs of juice from the canned pears, reserving 50 ml of the remaining juice. Slice the pear halves and arrange on top of the biscuits. Set aside.

To make the chocolate sauce, break up the chocolate into small pieces and place in a pan with the reserved 50 ml of pear juice. Melt over a low heat, then bring to a boil for about a minute, stirring continuously until it thickens a little. Remove from the heat and leave to cool. When cool, pour it over the pears until they are well covered with the sauce.

Beat the mascarpone, icing sugar and cream until smooth and spread this mixture on top of the chocolate sauce. Decorate with the almonds and delicate strips of angelica.

Citrus fruits have not figured much in the recipes given so far, but are prominent in the next recipe, which has a complex history. It first appeared, so far as we can ascertain, many years ago as an item by Delia Smith in the *BBC Good Food* magazine. It became a favourite of Margaret Little, who adapted it somewhat and eventually passed it on to us. We have tinkered further. So perhaps Delia Smith would rather not have it, in its present form, attributed to her. Let us leave it that whatever merit readers perceive in it should be credited to her, and any snags should be presumed to be our fault. The recipe serves 8 to 10.

CARAMELIZED ORANGE TRIFLE

FOR THE TRIFLE BASE: 5 trifle sponges; 2–3 tbs Seville orange marmalade; 150 ml Sercial Madeira (or sherry); 2 smallish bananas.

FOR THE CARAMEL ORANGES: 3 large Navel oranges; 2 tbs soft dark brown sugar; 1 tbs cognac.

FOR THE CUSTARD: 5 egg yolks ; 25 g caster sugar; 1 tsp cornflour; few drops pure vanilla extract; 425 ml double cream

FOR THE TOPPING: 300 ml double cream, whipped; 2 tbs lightly toasted and roughly chopped hazelnuts.

Split the sponges in half lengthways, spread each half with marmalade and then form them into sandwiches. Spread the top of each sandwich with more marmalade, then cut each across into three and arrange the pieces in the bottom of a 1.75 litre glass bowl. Make a few stabs in the sponges with a knife and pour the Madeira over them, distributing it evenly.

Grate and reserve the zest from one of the oranges. Pare skin and pith from all the oranges, then cut out the segments from between the membranes (fiddly work, some would use canned mandarin orange segments). Do this over a bowl to catch the juice (needed later). Halve the segments and place in a small bowl with the grated zest.

To make the caramel, dissolve the brown sugar and one tablespoon of the collected orange juice in a small pan over a gentle heat. As soon as the sugar crystals have dissolved, turn up the heat to caramelize the mixture – it is ready when it turns one shade darker and syrupy. Remove the pan from the heat and add the cognac, then pour the mixture over the orange segments and zest.

Make the custard by mixing the egg yolks, sugar, cornflour and vanilla extract in a bowl. Bring the cream up to simmering point in a pan and pour it over the egg mixture. Whisk well, return the egg mixture to the pan and reheat gently, still whisking, until the custard has thickened. Don't worry if it looks curdled at this stage; the cornflour will ensure that it becomes smooth once it is removed from the heat, as long as you keep whisking. Let the custard cool.

Meanwhile strain the pieces of orange segments, reserving the liquid. Arrange the orange pieces in among the sponge cakes in the trifle bowl. Slice the bananas thinly and scatter them into the bowl; you can push them down the sides as well. Then add the caramel juice to the custard and pour it on top of everything in the bowl.

Cover and chill for several hours before topping the trifle with the whipped cream and scattering it with the toasted hazelnuts. Serve well chilled.

Here is a special trifle, devised by Helen to celebrate the fiftieth issue of *PPC*, the journal of food history which Alan and Jane Davidson founded in 1979.

100 g boudoir biscuits; strawberry jam; 140 ml Cointreau or sweet sherry; 250 g halved or sliced strawberries, reserving a few for decoration; 1 strawberry or orange jelly; 6 macaroons, lightly crushed.

FOR THE CUSTARD: 565 ml double cream; 2 tbs sugar; 6 egg yolks; 2 tsp cornflour; 1 tsp vanilla essence (optional).

FOR THE SYLLABUB: 1 lemon; 3 tbs sweet or dry white wine; 2 tsp orange flower water; 75 g caster sugar; 280 ml double cream.

Sandwich the boudoir biscuits together with the jam in pairs and lay in the bottom of a glass bowl (preferably a decorative one). Sprinkle over the Cointreau or the sherry and allow it to soak into the biscuits. Cover with the strawberries.

Make the jelly (according to the packet instructions but with slightly less water, i.e. about 500 ml) and pour over the biscuits and fruits. Sprinkle the crushed macaroons on top and leave to set in a cool place.

Now make the custard. Heat the double cream in a saucepan. Blend the egg yolks, sugar and cornflour together in a basin and, when the cream is hot, pour it over the mixture, stirring constantly. Return the mixture to the saucepan and stir continuously over a low heat until the custard thickens.

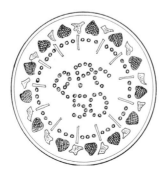

A top-down view of the PPC *50 Celebration Trifle, drawn by the artist Soun.*

Then remove it from the heat and allow it to cool a little. (If it starts to curdle, whisk vigorously until it is restored.) When sufficiently cool, pour it over the now set boudoir biscuits, fruit and jelly. Once again, allow to cool and to set completely before adding the syllabub.

Next, make the syllabub. Grate the rind of a lemon. Then squeeze out the juice from the lemon, and soak the rind in the juice for a couple of hours. Whip the cream until stiff. Add the sugar, wine and orange flower water to the lemon juice and then gently mix everything together to make a light frothy cream. Spread this syllabub over the custard.

Decorate according to your fancy with the strawberries and perhaps some silver dragées, toasted flaked almonds, angelica, or hundreds and thousands.

In accordance with Helen's family tradition, this recipe includes jelly. Helen's mother nearly always made her trifles with jelly; in this she may have been influenced by the fact that just after the war, in order to make ends meet, she worked for Rowntree's in York. Rowntree's were and are famous for their jellies.

In fact, the use of jelly in trifles was established long ago, in the eighteenth century (see page 24), and remains fairly common in modern times. For some people, however, this use is inappropriate. An example of the 'storm in a trifle bowl' which it may provoke was experienced by the present authors when Helen's recipe for the *PPC* Celebration Trifle was published. Its use of jelly provoked some strongly worded protests. Barbara Sobey and Damaris Hayman wrote:

> ... We had thought PPC a periodical devoted to the higher realms of cookery; this 'trifle' appears to be more suited to a school treat than a gastronome's table.
>
> Jelly? (packet jelly at that), fruit? cornflour in the custard? Dragées on top? and Hundreds and Thousands? (guaranteed to 'bleed' into the cream). And no ratafia biscuits. Oh dear.

In contrast, Phil Iddison in the Persian Gulf wrote in ardent support of the recipe in the form in which we gave it. He did, and does, have a difficulty over jelly, but this does not involve questioning, even to the slightest degree, the use of a packet of Rowntree's jelly; on the contrary, it consists simply in the fact that this product is unavailable in the market at Al Ain (Abu Dhabi)! He has had to resort to making jelly with local citrus fruits and agar agar. Nor does this fully describe his predicament. On top of these practical difficulties, he tells us that his wife Patsy actually belongs to the 'no jelly in any form' school of thought. Their difference of attitude is an entirely amiable one, thus conforming with Helen Saberi's original recommendation that people should be allowed, even encouraged, to do their own thing when making and decorating trifles.

CHAPTER SIX

TRIFLE IN THE NEW WORLDS:
THE AMERICAS AND AUSTRALASIA

The trifle found a ready welcome in the USA, and also in other overseas English-speaking countries including anglophone Canada, Australia, and New Zealand. Wherever it arrived it was likely to be adapted to use local ingredients – see for example the use of feijoas in the Green and Gold Trifle in David Burton's *Two Hundred Years of New Zealand Food & Cookery* (1982) and the Guava and Passion Fruit Trifle in Elizabeth Schneider's *Uncommon Fruits and Vegetables* (1986 and 2000). It might also veer off in unexpected directions; witness the trend in the USA towards the whole tribe of Tipsy Squires etc. which had an English origin but bloomed in greater abundance in the American climate.

Looking first at North America, we have trifles from the USA, and Canada, and (particularly interesting for the food historian) Mexico.

THE UNITED STATES

Although some unconventional trifles appeared later in the USA, as noted above, trifles had a conventional start in that country, as can be seen from Mrs Mary Randolph's famous trifle recipe of 1824 (below) and from the wording of the eulogy by that eminent American writer, Oliver Wendell Holmes (1861) who made reference to:

> That most wonderful object of domestic art called trifle ...
> with its charming confusion of cream and cake and almonds
> and jam and jelly and wine and cinnamon and froth.

MARY RANDOLPH'S TRIFLE

Mrs Randolph's book *The Virginia House-wife*, first published in 1824, and recently made available in a facsimile reprint with an introduction by Karen Hess (1984) is a mine of good things.

Her trifle recipe ends with a really useful tip on the choice of decorations.

TO MAKE A TRIFLE.

Put slices of Savoy cake or Naples biscuit at the bottom of a deep dish, wet it with white wine, and fill the dish nearly to the top with rich boiled custard; season half a pint of cream with white wine and sugar, whip it to a froth; as it rises, take it lightly off and lay it on the custard; pile it up high and tastely; decorate it with preserves of any kind, cut so thin as not to bear the froth down by its weight.

Another nineteenth-century publication, *Mrs Hill's Southern Practical Cookery and Receipt Book,* of which there is a facsimile reprint (reproducing the 1872 edition, edited by Annabella P. Hill, 1995), has a recipe for Trifle (given below because of its unusual features), but also exhibits the other tendency mentioned above, i.e. going off in an unexpected direction with a recipe for Gipsy Squire, which clearly belongs to the whole range of tipsy squires, tipsy parsons, tipsy lairds etc. which have adorned American cookery books. One cannot help wondering whether 'Gipsy Squire' is a misprint for 'Tipsy Squire' (the permutations and combinations are potentially almost infinite in number. There could, for example, be a Tipsy Hedgehog lurking somewhere in the literature or a Gipsy Parson, although we have so far traced neither of these.) Anyway, here are Mrs Hill's two recipes.

Trifle. – Beat the whites of four eggs to a stiff froth; whip a pint of rich cream on a flat dish with a silver fork or egg-beater until very solid; then mix the two in a bowl, adding alternately cream and egg, a spoonful at a time; flavor to taste. Serve in a glass stand, putting in a layer of cream, then one of almond macaroons or meringues. Prepare this just before serving.

Gipsy Squire. – Saturate with Sherry wine a thin sponge-cake. Ornament the top with blanched almonds, sticking them in with the points upwards and tastily arranged. Half fill a large glass bowl with a good boiled custard, and carefully place the cake on the top of the custard, taking care that the bowl used is of a circumference somewhat larger than that of the cake.

In contrast, Marion Harland (*Marion Harland's Complete Cook Book*, 1903) lavishes mainstream trifle recipes upon her readers (although she does have one Tipsy Pudding). Besides the Peach Trifle given below, she offers a pound cake trifle, a raspberry trifle, and a rhubarb trifle (actually more like a fool).

Peach Trifle

Boil together for five minutes one cupful of sugar and one cupful of water. Put into this one quart of pared peaches. Stir slowly until tender. When almost cold press them through a sieve. Line a deep glass dish with stale sponge cake dipped in sherry. Spread over this the cold peach pulp. Flavor one and a half cupfuls of thick sweet cream with two tablespoonfuls of powdered sugar and one teaspoonful, each, of vanilla and lemon and whip until thick and solid. Pour this into [onto] the peaches and let it stand until very cold.

[HELEN COMMENTS: 'When I tested this recipe I took a short cut with the peaches – instead of pressing them through a sieve, I sliced them thinly, poached them and then placed the slices with a little of the syrup on top of the cake layer. I found that four medium peaches was about right and that the recipe served four people.']

There are two trifles in *200 years of Charleston Cooking* (first published in 1931) by Blanche Rhett, Lettie Gay and Helen Woodward. The one which we reproduce below was taken by these three ladies from *The Carolina Housewife* by Sarah Rutledge, writing in 1847 as 'A Lady of Charleston' (available in a facsimile reprint edited by a descendant, 1979). It is interesting to note that one change was made by the ladies. They introduced a reference to 'wine flavouring', since their book first came out during the Prohibition years. But they did allow for using some actual wine as well as wine flavouring.

So here it is, a recipe of 1847 brought back into circulation in 1931. By the way, we recommend the advice in the last paragraph, i.e. covering the macaroon and sponge cake base with a layer of custard.

Trifle II

This is a rather elaborate dessert with a pronounced wine flavor. Lay in the bottom of a glass dessert bowl a quarter of a pound of macaroons and a few slices of sponge cake. Wet them thoroughly with sweet wine flavoring.

Whip together the following ingredients: One pint of cream, one-half cup of milk, one cup of Teneriffe wine (port wine flavoring will do as a substitute), the grated rind of one lemon and the juice of half a lemon, and one-eighth teaspoon each of cinnamon, nutmeg and mace, adding sugar to taste. As the froth arises, take it off and lay it upon the cake until the dish is full.

"A custard may be put first upon the cake" the recipe suggests, "and the froth laid lightly upon that." This makes an even richer dessert but the flavor is delightful.

We conclude this section on American trifles with two glimpses of their status in the twentieth century. First, a quotation which relates to the famous British-born Hollywood film star and director, Ida Lupino. (Her beauty was striking, as was the skill with which she acted 'tough' parts, e.g. the accomplice of safe-cracker Bogart in *High Sierra*, the singer in *Road House*, a prison governor, etc. Against this background it is a real surprise to find her arranging flowers in crystal bowls for her guests!)

Secondly, a passage written by M.F.K. Fisher, the greatest of American cookery writer of the century; it comes from her book *With Bold Knife and Fork* (1969).

In his biography of Ida Lupino (1996), William Donati has this to say:

The Haywards [Ida Lupino and her husband, Louis Hayward] preferred to entertain at home and employed a cook and a houseman on a full-time basis. Guests were treated to candlelit dinners on their eight-foot antique oak table. The menu was usually roast beef, potatoes, and Ida's favorite dessert, trifle, a sponge cake soaked in sherry and covered with custard, whipped cream, nuts, raisins, and fruit. Ida disliked cooking but supervised the meals. She personally arranged the table settings, filling crystal bowls with daffodils and roses. ...

The evocative and charming book by Betty Goodwin, entitled *Hollywood Du Jour – Lost Recipes of Legendary Hollywood Haunts*, 1993, describes an English pub which existed from 1937 to 1987 on Sunset Boulevard in the Beverley Hills area and was frequented by many 'denizens of filmland' and notables such as Scott FitzGerald and Somerset Maugham. A recipe is given for the 'Trifle Pudding' served at the Cock 'N Bull (that was its name) and it may not be altogether fanciful to suppose that this bore some relation to Ida Lupino's trifle.

The trifle was made by breaking into halves and mixing together a quarter pound of almond macaroons and a quarter pound of lady fingers, spreading raspberry jam generously around the inside walls of the glass trifle bowl and sticking about half the cookie combination to the inside of the bowl. A custard sauce is then made, incorporating cornstarch and egg yolks plus sherry and brandy. The remainder of the cookie mixture is mixed into the sauce, which is poured into the bowl. More jam is dotted over the top and, after a night in the refrigerator the trifle is decorated with whipped cream and cherries.

Our passage from M.F.K. Fisher reads as follows:

A trifle can be a pretty thing, and it needs a pretty dish, one with a stem. I have one which is properly a Swedish vase, standing about eighteen inches tall, with fluted edges, veins of color in the glass, and other flighty and endearing qualities. It is predestined, once or twice a year but most often around Christmas, to hold a monumental chilled pudding made from sponge cake, macaroons, jam, brandy or whatever liquor seems indicated, custards, whipped cream.

Mrs Fisher went on to explain that she took great pains to procure the best possible canned fruits (of various kinds) which might or might not (for 'innocent' trifles) be marinated in kirschwasser or brandy. Somebody 'then lines the almost transparent Swedish bowl with the beautiful fruits, whose colors take on stained-glass patterns, heady or pure'. Instead of having sponge cake or crumbled macaroons in the trifle, she served delicate little biscuits at the side. For the custard, crème anglaise or crème pâtissière, with sour cream or flavoured sweet cream folded in. On top of this she might form a dome of whipped cream. Then: 'Our trifles have been ornamented with everything from slices of hazelnut sticking out like spines between rows of brandied raisins, to animals carved from peach halves, to slivered ginger with a Japanese midget's parasol at the top.'

CANADA

Here we have studied with interest *The New Cook Book by The Ladies of Toronto*, revised edition, 1906. The ladies have a 'traditional' trifle, but also a lemon trifle which is really a sort of syllabub and two trifles containing figs; the first which is called Fig Trifle is also more like syllabub or fool and contains walnuts. The second trifle with figs, the recipe for which follows, is a bit vague as to amounts and lacks instructions for making almond custard, for which Helen has therefore supplied a proven recipe of her own.

TRIFLE

Sponge cake, soaked in sherry wine; chopped figs and a pint of almond custard, large cup of strawberry jam, one pint of cream, whipped, for top.

Our adapted recipe, which serves 6 to 8, is as follows:

Fig Trifle

8 slices of sponge cake; strawberry jam; 8 tbs sweet sherry; 8 figs, preferably fresh; almond custard ; 300 ml whipping cream.

FOR THE ALMOND CUSTARD: 50 g almonds; 3 egg yolks; 500 ml whole milk; 2 level tbs cornflour; 3 tbs sugar; 1 tbs rosewater (optional).

Line the bottom of a crystal bowl with the slices of sponge cake and spread strawberry jam liberally over them. Sprinkle the cake with the sherry adding enough so as to soak the cakes. Peel and quarter the figs and lay on top of the cakes. Set to one side.

Now make the almond custard. Blanch the almonds and remove the skins. Bring 110 ml water to the boil and pour over the almonds in a bowl and leave to soak for about 15 minutes. Put the almonds and their water into an electric blender and chop very finely. Strain the almond milk through a double layer of muslin into a bowl, squeezing the cloth to extract as much almond milk as possible. Set to one side.

Mix the cornflour with a little of the milk into a smooth paste. Beat in the 3 egg yolks and stir in the sugar. Heat the remaining milk to boiling point, then slowly, and stirring constantly, add to the cornflour and egg mixture. Return the custard to the pan and stir continuously over a low heat until the custard has thickened. Add the rosewater, milk of almonds and simmer gently for a couple more minutes, then remove from the heat and set aside to cool.

When the custard has cooled pour over the cakes and fruit and allow to set completely.

Whip the cream, with a little icing sugar, and add to the top of the trifle.

In the southern hemisphere we have selected two trifles from Australia, where English cookery traditions flourished with surprising vigour in the centuries which followed the first settlements, and where they still play an important part in the rich multi-ethnic cuisine of the continent.

The Cookery Book of Good and Tried Receipts (12th edn. 1912, first published in Sydney, 1895) was also known as 'The Presbyterian Cookery Book', which probably gives us a clue to the reason for its recipe for 'lemon trifle' containing no alcohol. In fact, the idea of giving a trifle a predominant lemon flavour is an interesting one and produces a good result.

HELEN WRITES: In the version below I have slightly modified the list of ingredients and the initial instructions in the light of my own tests of the recipe, but have retained the rest of the instructions (in double quotes) in the original pleasing prose of the author.

LEMON TRIFLE

250 g sponge cake; 1 litre whole milk; 3 large eggs (whites and yolks separate); 7 heaped tbs caster sugar; 1 lemon (all the juice and ¼ of the rind very finely grated); lemon essence.

Cut the cake into slices and arrange in a deep glass dish. Take one teacupful of the milk and heat it. Pour it over the cake slices and leave to soak. "Well beat the yolks of the eggs, and stir with them four tablespoons of the caster sugar. Heat the rest of the milk and pour it upon the eggs by degrees, stirring all the time; return it to the saucepan, and continue stirring till it thickens; let it cool a little, add the strained juice of the lemon, and pour over the sponge cake. When perfectly cold heap upon it a meringue made of the whites of the eggs whipped to a stiff froth, sweetened with the [remaining] sugar, and flavoured with the essence of lemon and the rind. The meringue should be made just before serving."

As a ballroom dance, the tango achieved its first peak of popularity in the 1920s, which fits in with what we know about the dating of this recipe. The title conjures up a vision of elegant figures swooping and swerving around an art deco dance floor before settling at a table and enjoying this delicacy from art deco tableware. Our source, *The Barossa Cookery Book*, is one of those which has lived on through many generations and many successive editions, often undated and thus providing additional fields of research for bibliographers. What we have is the twenty-seventh edition, one of the undated ones but probably *circa* 1980. It appears to be a straightforward reprint of one of the earlier editions, probably around 1931, a good tango year. The author of the recipe is identified as 'Mrs J.T. Kleemann, Tanunda'. Here is her text:

TANGO TRIFLE

Sponge fingers, bananas, macaroons, 1 packet vanilla custard powder, cream, hundreds and thousands.

Method: Put some sponge fingers together with jam, allow two for each trifle. Chop up and arrange in the bottom of Melba glasses. Moisten cakes with equal quantities of sherry and pineapple juice, cover with a layer of vanilla custard. Pile up with chopped banana, or chopped pineapple and banana. Cover with whipped cream and rim with macaroons or ratafias. Sprinkle with hundreds and thousands.

[HELEN COMMENTS: In interpreting this I took my pineapple and pineapple juice from a small can of pineapple; I used 4 tbs sherry; was careful to use packet custard, as recommended; and concluded that one large or two smaller bananas were needed, and 140 ml whipping cream.]

TRINIDAD

Quite a number of British dishes turn up in the Caribbean region, in versions adapted to local ingredients. One example, given in summary form here is described by Dave Dewitt and Mary Jane Wilan (*Callaloo, Calypso and Carnival – the Cuisines of Trinidad and Tobago*) as 'fairly complicated, but fun'. They explain that trifles are usually made in Trinidad with canned fruit cocktail, but that they prefer to select from the tropical fruits locally available.

TRINI TROPICAL TRIFLE

Make a custard flavoured with vanilla and let it cool. Then spread a thin layer of it over the bottom of a deep glass dish. Distribute over this base cubes of sponge cake soaked in a mixture of 4 parts sherry to 2 parts of West Indian rum. Spread over this a fruit filling of diced mango, pineapple and banana, prepared in a little sugar syrup. Over this filling spread the remaining custard, and then a plentiful amount of whipped cream. Decorate with fresh cherries, pitted and halved, sprinkle with slivered almonds, and refrigerate for at least half an hour before serving.

LATIN AMERICA

Not all the trifles which are found in other continents have a British origin. It seems clear that some of the trifle-type dishes of continental Europe were themselves exported across the seas, bobbing up in various places where English culinary influence was zero. A prime example is Mexico, where there is a minor but flourishing branch of the trifle family. Some believe that this may be due to the influence of Roman Catholic nuns, from Italy rather than Spain (where there is no tradition of trifle-like confections).

Key words in Mexican trifle terminology are *Capirotada* and *Ante* (plural *Antes*). The former is dealt with in the Glossary, since it is a real chameleon of a word, defying classification. The latter is a wide-ranging category of dishes, given unity by the nature of the base which supports them all. As the wonderful reference book called *Nuevo Cocinero Mexicano en forma de Diccionario* (1888 edition, published as a facsimile reprint in 1986) puts it:

> ANTE. By this name are designated an innumerable range of dishes, of various substances mixed with sugar syrup and disposed on beds of soft sponge cake, with various different kinds of decoration.

When the base is used under layers of fruit and custard and decorated with slivers of candied fruit (often, in Mexico, *acitrón* – see Glossary – from the biznaga cactus, but citrus fruits, including citron are perfectly acceptable), the result is a trifle.

According to Brenda Garza Sada (personal communication), *antes* of this sort are known mostly around Mexico City. A ladyfinger-type cookie, or cake, may be used, drenched in syrup, with chopped Mexican fruit (fresh like *mamey* – see Glossary – or the *acitrón* already mentioned). They usually have layers of pastry cream or marzipan.

Brenda Garza Sada sent us numerous recipes, but the one which caught our eyes the most was *Ante de Yemas*, which appeared as 'Mexican Trifle' in the book *The Mexican Gourmet* by Shelton Wiseman and José N. Iturriaga (1995), with recipes by Maria Dolores Torres Yzábal. The authors introduce the recipe as follows:

> The European tradition of *antes*, or trifle, came to Mexico in the nineteenth century. Recipe books and manuscripts from that era describe *antes* as a type of bread soaked in wine and layered with *natillas* (milk custard), fruit, or nuts. In this dish the candied *acitrón* is made from cactus, which is a typical Mexican touch.

ANTE DE YEMAS 'Mexican Trifle'
(to serve 10)

FOR THE PASTRY CREAM: 250 ml milk; 3 egg yolks; 125 g sugar; 3 tsp cornstarch [cornflour]; 1 tbs butter; 1 tsp vanilla extract;

FOR THE SYRUP: 250 ml water; 185 g sugar; 125 ml dry sherry; 24–30 lady fingers; 75 g pine nuts; 75 g acitrón (crystallized biznaga cactus)

To make the pastry cream: Heat the milk in a small saucepan over a low heat. In a small bowl, beat the egg yolks with the sugar until thick. Mix in the cornstarch and slowly stir in the milk.

Pour the mixture into a clean saucepan and cook over a low heat, stirring constantly with a wooden spoon until the mixture comes to a boil and thickens (the lumps will smooth out as you stir). Remove the pan from the heat and add the butter and vanilla, blending until the butter has melted. Cover with plastic wrap until the mixture cools.

To make the syrup: Bring the water and sugar to a boil and simmer for 5 minutes. Let cool, then stir in the sherry.

Dip the lady fingers in the syrup one by one. Layer half of them in a round (23 x 4 cm) serving dish and top with half the pastry cream. Sprinkle with half the pine nuts and *acitrón*. Repeat the layering with the remaining ingredients and serve.

[COMMENTS BY ALAN AND HELEN: The proportion of custard to lady fingers is a little different from the English traditional trifle and we can suggest that, if desired, amounts can be doubled for the pastry cream. Mexicans also have a very sweet tooth and the proportion of sugar in the pastry cream can be reduced if wished.]

The so-called 'Viceroy's Dessert' (*Postre de Virrey*) has been described as a typical upper-class dish in Mexico of the late nineteenth century. The lavish use of egg yolks recalls the sweet confections of convents in Spain, brought with them by Spanish nuns when they went overseas to found new convents abroad. However, this particular confection does not echo anything we have been able to trace in the homeland.

The Viceroy's dessert is a multi-layered job, which needs to be prepared in a deep dish, not too great in diameter since otherwise the ingredients will be used up in too few layers.

The recipe given by Elisabeth Lambert Ortiz in *The Complete Book of Mexican Cooking* (1967) and the other recipe we have used, from *Mexican Cook Book devoted to American Homes* (by Josefina Velazquez de Leon, 11th edn., 1978) are quite close to each other, but each has its own attractive features which we have embodied in this composite version.

THE 'CUSTARD'. Boil 3 cups (675 grams) granulated sugar in 1 cup (225 ml) of water until it reaches the thread stage (230°C on the candy thermometer). Cool it, then add 16 lightly beaten egg yolks and a teaspoon of ground cinnamon. Cook the mixture over a low flame until it has thickened like a custard. Stir ½ cup (110 ml) sherry into it.

THE CREAM. Whip one cup (225 ml) whipping cream to stiff peaks. Beat 4 egg whites with 2 tablespoons of confectioner's sugar until stiff, then fold this into the whipped cream together with 1 tablespoon of brandy.

THE CAKE. You need a generous quantity of sponge cake, or a dozen or so small sponge cakes weighing approximately 450 g, sliced fairly thinly (1 cm thick) and divided into pieces which can be used as 'crazy paving'. At least three layers of this are required. Each layer will be moistened (not soaked) with more sherry and thinly spread with a jam of your choice (apricot, for example).

CONSTRUCTION. Cover the bottom of your dish with a

first layer of cake, as described above. A layer of the 'custard' goes on top of this, then another layer of cake, followed by a layer of the whipped cream. You now have four layers in all. Repeat the sequence with four more, in the same sequence. If your dish is relatively small in diameter you may have enough ingredients to repeat a third time. In any case, you finish up with a layer of whipped cream.

DECORATION. This being a New World dish, it is fitting to decorate it with a New World discovery, grated chocolate. But our general principle of 'decorate as you please' holds good here, and you may prefer flaked almond or hundreds and thousands (to be added at the last moment) called coloured candy sprinkles in Mexico.

Finally, an intriguing item from Shirley Lomax Brooks' excellent book *Argentina Cooks!* She describes it, correctly, as an English-type trifle; but it has a Spanish name which is converted from the Italian name *Zuppa Inglese* (for the meaning of which see page 105). An etymological tangle but a delicious dish.

SOPA INGLESA

'Many English settled in Argentina when they came to build the railroads. They yearned for English food, not the barbaric fare eaten by their Argentine hosts. Somehow, they managed to keep a stiff upper lip until the next ship came in with tinned pound cake and a dusty bottle of Jerez sherry.'

1 shortcake or pound cake; ½ cup Oloroso sherry; dulce de leche *(see below); 1 teaspoon vanilla; 2 teaspoons sugar; ½ pint heavy cream.*

Cover the bottom of a deep transparent serving bowl with a layer of shortcake or pound cake, about ¾ inches thick. Pour ¼ cup sherry over the cake. Spread a layer of *dulce de leche* on top, about ¼ inch thick. Add another layer of cake and sprinkle it with the remaining ¼ cup sherry. Add vanilla and sugar to the cream and whip it until it holds a peak. Spread a thick layer of whipped cream over the cake. When served, sprinkle the top with additional sherry.

Dulce de Leche – or milk pudding – is an Argentine staple. In the old days, home cooks made it in quantity because it keeps indefinitely and they wanted to always have some on hand. The recipe given here is the traditional one.

Combine 2 cups of milk, ¾ cup of sugar and a dash of baking soda in a saucepan. Bring the mixture to a boil. Lower the heat and keep the mixture barely at a simmer for about 2 ½ hours, stirring occasionally. When the mixture forms a soft ball in cold water, remove it from the heat and stir in 1 tsp vanilla. Cool before using.

CHAPTER SEVEN

TRIFLES IN CONTINENTAL EUROPE AND ELSEWHERE

What happened to the trifle when it sailed overseas to non-English-speaking countries? It got into France as 'Bagatelle', the name chosen by the baffled French translator of the English authors Collingwood and Woollams (1810) to head their recipe for this item, evidently incomprehensible to the French. (This was the subject of comments by Elizabeth David in her essay on 'Syllabubs and Fruit Fools', reprinted in *An Omelette and a Glass of Wine*, 1984; she thought that the French name restored to the trifle some of its 'lost charm'.)

Reverberations don't seem to have amounted to much. But the illustrious, and one of the most respected of French culinary writers, Jules Gouffé in *Le Livre de Pâtisserie* of 1873 included a chapter on 'Pâtisserie étrangère', in which we find a recipe entitled 'Mousse à l'Anglaise', which we give a translation of below:

Mousse à l'Anglaise

Trim and cut up sponge cake into slices 1 cm thick. Arrange them in two layers in the bottom of a deep dish. Place on top a layer of macaroons and pour over the whole 4 decilitres [400 ml] of Madeira. Let this be absorbed by the sponge cake.

Prepare a custard with 8 egg yolks, 3 decilitres [300 ml] of cream and milk, and a dessertspoon [cuillerée] of sugar, and flavouring as you wish. Heat this, without allowing it to boil, until thickened. Let it cool, then pass it through a muslin and pour it over the sponge cakes and macaroons to form a layer 2 cm thick above them.

Spread lightly over the custard a little apricot jam, then cover the whole with a good layer of whipped cream, sweetened and flavoured. Decorate the top with [more] whipped cream, coloured rose or chocolate.

The example set by Gouffé, in adopting an English trifle recipe, does not seem to have been followed by other French writers or chefs. Nor is there much evidence to suggest that Gouffé's example affected people in other European countries. It is true that in the greatest (anyway the biggest) Swedish cookery book, that by Hagdahl (1896), there is a recipe, which is quite close to Gouffé's, under the title 'Lappri (Fr. Mousse à l'anglaise. Eng. Trifle)', but this seems to have been an isolated example. (The Swedish word *Lappri* does in fact mean trifle in the general sense of something small and insignificant.)

What we do find in the Nordic countries is a group of recipes for a dish which has a family resemblance to trifle but is presented under names which translate as 'veiled maidens' or 'peasant girl with a veil', or, (the Icelandic *Bóndadóttir með blæju*) peasant's daughter with a veil. These are mysterious names and the mystery has sometimes been deepened for English readers by a mis-spelling which would in translation produce 'soiled maiden' instead of 'veiled maiden' in an otherwise admirable book about apples published in the 1980s. However, it seems that the veil, at least, can be explained by reference to the topping of whipped cream which almost invariably adorns the dish. In Norway, such recipes were current in the latter part of the nineteenth century, but the example given on page 84 is a recent version for which Henry Notaker, the leading food historian in Norway, is responsible.

The 'veiled maidens' are not the only Nordic phenomena in this field. There is a clear tendency to use certain fruits, especially apples, raspberries and sometimes rhubarb. There are also various recipes which call for the trifle-like dish to be made in a 'vase'. Nordic experts assure us that this does mean something shaped like a flower vase. Making the reasonable assumption that this would be of glass, one can see that it would exhibit the multi-layering of the dish very successfully.

There is a further point to be noted from Denmark. The Danish *æblekage* means 'apple cake', but in a broader sense than is usual in English. In fact, it seems that it can be used to refer to Danish 'veiled maidens', and it is certainly true that these maidens exist in

Denmark (where names such as *tilslørede bondepiger* are used, almost the same as the Norwegian *Tilslørte bondepiker*), whether or not they shelter (as they usually do nowadays) under the umbrella of 'apple cake'. It is with a sense of relief that we discover that way back in 1850 Fru Mangor author of one of the most important early Danish cookery books, had a recipe for something called 'Trifli', which was much closer to an English trifle than any of the veiled maidens. (Incidentally, it is also remarkably similar to the Icelandic recipe for *triffli* which we give on page 85, and may well have been the basis on which the latter was developed.)

Although the term 'trifli' is still in use in Denmark it is uncommon. Some scholars believe that the 'trifles' of Denmark arrived from a German source, perhaps especially from coastal areas. Whether this is so or not, it prompts prior consideration of what Germans have actually done in this area of activity.

By the way, the map below shows the Scandinavian region, which is the heartland of the veiled peasant maidens and their like. Research remains to be done on the extent to which they may have infiltrated the Baltic States and perhaps even the western part of the Russian Federation, also, the likely appearance of their offspring in other parts of the world to which Scandinavian people have emigrated.

In an important contribution to a discussion of trifles in *PPC* 51, Lesley Chamberlain remarks that the extent of culinary interchanges between England and Germany across the North Sea needs further research, but that the recipe which follows, and which is associated with Thomas Mann and the port of Lübeck, and more particularly with his 1903 novel *Buddenbrooks*, is suggestive. However, she also observes that Sybil Gräfin Schönfeld (who in her book *Bei Thomas Mann zu Tisch* recreates the dishes mentioned in the novel) does not indicate that this was considered to be, like the plum cake for which a recipe is also given, an importation from England.

Plettenpudding

4–6 slices leftover plain cake; 1 glass sherry; 1 glass raspberry jam; 1 pack fresh or frozen raspberries; ¼ litre milk; ¾ litre cream; 6 egg yolks; 125 g sugar; 1 sachet powdered gelatine or 6 leaves; 1 dessertspoon vanilla sugar; almond macaroons to decorate.

Steep the cake slices in sherry in a glass bowl. Stir the jam to a pouring consistency and drip over the cake, followed by the fruit. Meanwhile over a bain-marie make a custard with the milk, ½ litre of the cream, the egg yolks and sugar. Dissolve the gelatine as directed, add to the thickened custard and allow to cool before pouring over the raspberries. Finish the trifle with a layer of the remaining cream, whipped stiff with the vanilla sugar. Decorate with macaroons.

So now we come to recipes from Denmark and the Nordic countries.

HINDEBÆRSKUM MED FRUGTLIKER
Raspberry foam with fruit liqueur
(to serve four)

This is a Danish recipe given to us by Svein Fosså, who says that he believes that the recipe originally came from Germany. Although the name does not suggest that this is a trifle, one can tell from the ingredients that it is quite a close relation. The liqueur recommended is German: Schlehen Feuer, meaning 'sloe fire'.

250 ml whipping cream
12 macaroons
250 g raspberries
4 tablespoons fruit-based liqueur
sugar

Crush the macaroons coarsely and distribute evenly into four sundae glasses. Sprinkle 1 tablespoon of the liqueur over each of the four portions.

Purée the raspberries (setting a few aside for decoration) and add sugar to taste. Whip the cream and set some aside for decoration. Mix the rest with the raspberry purée. Distribute in the four glasses and decorate with the remainder of the whipped cream and some whole berries.

Our Norwegian recipe, for Veiled Maidens, comes from a brochure compiled by Henry Notaker for the Royal Norwegian Ministry of Foreign Affairs. As we have already indicated, there are many variations of this recipe all over the Nordic countries. Illustrating some of the variations in Norway, Henry tells us that Veiled Maidens etc. are often made with a base of pumpernickel rather than biscuits; that a little lemon juice can be added to the apples whilst cooking; that raspberry or redcurrant jelly can be interspersed between the layers or used as a final decoration on top of the cream; and that grated chocolate can be used instead of toasted almonds.

Tilslørte Bondepiker
Veiled Maidens

4–5 cooking apples or 200–300 ml apple purée
50 g sugar
50 ml water
200–300 g biscuit crumbs (or dried breadcrumbs)
2–3 tbs sugar
2–3 tbs butter
300 ml (approx) whipping cream
100 g coarsely chopped toasted almonds

Peel, core and chop the apples. Cook with the sugar and water until just soft. Cool. Melt the butter in a hot frying pan. Mix the crumbs and sugar with the butter and fry until the mixture is crisp and golden. Whip the cream. Place the apple purée, cream and crumbs in layers in a glass dish. Garnish with the almonds.

Iceland is one country where the history of trifles has been taken seriously, notably by Nanna Rögnvaldardóttir, author of *Icelandic Food & Cookery* (Hippocrene Books, New York, 2001). She tells us that trifle probably came to Iceland from Denmark in the late nineteenth century. Its Icelandic name, *triffli* (with variant spellings such as *trifl*), first appeared in print around that time. Some recipes for trifle in the first half of the twentieth century have included 'a shockingly large amount of rum or sherry'. Later in the century, the classic work by Helga Sigurðardóttir, *Matur og drykkur*, appeared, including a rather vague recipe for rhubarb trifle (stale cake in cubes, rhubarb purée, custard, whipped cream, no wine or alcohol) and two additional recipes which seem to be trifles although not so labelled in the book (one is called Gentlemen's Dessert, presumably because it includes a little wine, and the other Macaroon Dessert no. 1). The most recent edition of Helga's book, published long after her death, has a version that includes fresh fruit, and the name has been Frenchified by another hand to *trifflé*.

As for its present status, Nanna says: 'Trifle, although well-known, is very much an old-fashioned dessert in Iceland; old-fashioned, upper-class and Christmassy.' The recipe provided by Nanna for our use is a rhubarb trifle:

ÖMMUTRIFFLI
(Grandmother's Trifle)

400 ml milk
1 vanilla bean, split
1 egg
3 egg yolks
75 g sugar, or to taste
125 g macaroons
4–5 tbs sherry or port
150 ml rhubarb jam, not too sweet
250 ml whipping cream
25 g chocolate, grated or chopped

First make the custard: Heat the milk to the boil with the vanilla bean, then remove from heat and let stand for a few minutes. Whisk the whole egg and the yolks with the sugar until golden and frothy. Remove the vanilla bean and pour the milk gradually into the egg mixture, whisking thoroughly.

Pour the custard back into the saucepan and whisk at very low heat until thickened. Cool the custard.

Crumble the macaroons roughly and spread them on the bottom of a nice glass bowl. Drizzle with sherry, then spoon the jam over the macaroons. Pour the cooled custard over the jam and refrigerate until set.

Decorate with whipped cream and chocolate.

Many of the Icelandic recipes include a cooked custard that is further stiffened with gelatine, an unusual feature. And most of them have either jam (rhubarb, blueberry, strawberry) or cooked fruit (rhubarb or prunes, usually). Some have no alcohol at all, some have undefined 'wine', some sherry or rum.

Moving over to Central Europe, we found little evidence of true trifles. In Austria we had a tantalizing glimpse (from Josephine Bacon, 1988) of something of a quasi-trifling nature: *Punschtorte*, described by Josephine as 'an Austrian version of Tipsy Cake', and highly complicated, the sort of thing one prefers to leave to the skill of Austrian pastry chefs. As for Hungary, similar comments might be applied to the Malakoff Cream Torte (*Malakoff-Krèmtorta*) described by George Lang (1971), except of course that the preparation would be entrusted to a pastry chef of Budapest. This latter item must exist elsewhere in Central and Eastern Europe, since Lang explains that it originated in Russia and 'was probably brought back by French chefs and then copied by other European chefs.' It does sound delicious.

However, we have been told of a Hungarian confection which is much more like a true trifle, and of which a slightly adapted version is given below. Ann Semple, of Toronto, tells us that the recipe comes from her cleaning lady, Marta Scheffer, and is roughly translated from an old Hungarian cookbook. 'The book is entitled *Srakácskönyv* or something of that sort, was published in Budapest in 1956, and the word itself means "Cookbook," according to Marta.' 1956 was of course the year of the uprising in Hungary, which caused the flight of Marta's family to Canada.

ANYÓSTORTA
(Mother-in-Law's Torte)

INGREDIENTS: 25 lady fingers; 250 ml milk; 50 g sugar ; 50 ml rum; 100 g raisins or candied fruit; 300 ml whipping cream.

CUSTARD: 1 litre milk; 4 egg yolks; 75 g flour; 15 g cocoa; 80 g sugar; ½ vanilla bean.

First of all make a custard in the usual way, with the 1 litre milk, egg yolks, flour, cocoa, sugar and vanilla bean. When smooth and thick remove the vanilla bean and allow to cool.

Mix the 250 ml milk and the sugar together in a bowl. Dip half of the ladyfingers in this mixture until moist and place in a glass bowl. Sprinkle with half of the rum. Then spoon on a layer of the custard. Over the custard sprinkle some of the raisins.

Make a second layer in the same manner.

Whip the cream and pipe it over the top of the *torta*.

ANGLO-INDIAN RECIPES

We now travel much further eastwards, to India, where the trifle became embedded in the standard menu of the social circle of Anglo-India in the days of the Raj. This is clear from, for example, E.M. Forster's *In a Passage to India* (1924) quoted by Brigid Allen (1994):

> And sure enough they did drive away from the club in a few minutes, and they did dress, and to dinner came Miss Derek and the McBrydes, and the menu was: Julienne soup full of bullety bottled peas, pseudo-cottage bread, fish full of branching bones, pretending to be plaice, more bottled peas with the cutlets, trifle, sardines on toast: the menu of Anglo-India ...

It is also interesting that during the nineteenth century some prominent English cookery writers (notably Mrs Rundell and Mrs Beeton) offered recipes for what they called an 'Indian trifle' – see page 30. Those trifles, however, in no way resemble what seems to be the traditional trifle of the Anglo-Indian kitchen, exemplified in the following recipe which comes from *Indian Domestic Economy*, by Dr R. Riddell, 1871.

TRIFLE

Cover the bottom of your dish with sponge-cakes or Naples biscuits divided into quarters; add some broken macaroons or ratafia cakes, just wet them through with sweet white wine or any other; cover the macaroons with raspberry jam or any other jam with some guava jelly; then pour over a rich thick custard, and cover the whole with a whipt cream as high as you can place it; sprinkle trifle comfits on the top, or garnish with different coloured sweetmeats.

Make your whip as follows: – Mix in a large bowl a quarter of a pound of finely-sifted sugar, the juice of two lemons, some of the peel grated fine, two table-spoonsful of brandy or noyeau and one of sweet wine, and a pint and a half of good cream; whisk the whole well, and take off the froth as it rises with a skimmer, and lay it on a sieve; continue to whisk it till you have enough to cover your trifle.

Obs.- A little noyeau or marischino [maraschino] may be added to the sponge-cake; in fact, it may be flavoured as fancy directs, and covered with everlasting syllabub.

However, the Anglo-Indian kitchen did not deal exclusively in traditional trifles; the tribe of 'tipsy' items also put in an appearance there; see, for an example page 100 in the chapter on Trifling Relations. What is more interesting is the emergence of a really distinctive item, Snow Eggs for Trifles, also in Dr Riddell's book.

SNOW EGGS FOR TRIFLES, &C.

Beat the whites of eight eggs until they form a very thick froth, which will take at least half an hour; put a pint and a half of milk to boil; when it boils place upon its surface as many table-spoonsful of the whipt whites of eggs as will stand upon it without touching each other; as each spoonful becomes cooked and assumes the appearance of snow, take it off, and put on another until all the whip is done; as you take off the snow from the milk, put it on a hair sieve to drain; when all the snow is done, add to the milk a bit of lemon-peel and sugar enough to sweeten it well; as soon as it has acquired the flavour of the lemon-peel, stir into it the yolks of the eight eggs beaten up with a tablespoonful of orange-flower water; when of proper consistency, but not so thick as cream, pour it into a cream-dish, and use it as directed for trifle, ornamenting the snow with thin slices of red currant jelly.

A hint of the ancestry of this frothy item is provided by a work which appeared some 30 years earlier: *The Magazine of Domestic*

Economy, vol 4, 1839, to which Laura Mason has kindly drawn our attention. It is an arresting piece of prose.

EGG-SNOW TRIFLE.–When white-of-egg is beat up into a very light froth, and in this state ladled spoonful by spoonful into boiling water, it immediately sets into a beautifully firm and white sponge having the appearance of snow. This garnish (as it may be considered) of the richer material it envelopes, is a favourite preparation of the French and German cookery, but considerable precaution and address are required to effect the preliminary object of obtaining the beaten froth in a successful manner. The French authors, with characteristic nonchalance, simply tell us that we *are* to do it, while the Germans more modestly condescend to instruct us in the elementary mode of proceeding. They inform us, first, that it is *essential* that the basin in which the chafing of this Scylla and Charybdis in miniature is to be excited, should be free from any moisture or the slightest *greasiness* (this calls to our remembrance, and also explains and illustrates a conjuror's trick in a little black-letter necromantic book of the middle-ages, "to prevent a tapster from raising a froth on the ale in his tankard," by rubbing the upper inside-rim with a greasy red-herring); and that to ensure success even a new vessel should be employed; next that the white must be beat in waves to one side of the basin with a thin flat slice of wood or a stiff rod, or whirled round in rapid eddies by means of a whisk, until it becomes as white as snow, and so firm that it remains fixed while the pot is turned upside down; that the eggs should be new-laid, and the whites scrupulously separated from any admixture of yolk, and the egg-snow prepared only just as wanted for table, as it soon subsides, becomes thin, and with further beating refuses again to assume the snowy form.

According to the testimony of James Bishop, one of many expatriates working in Kuwait, the trifle has penetrated the northern part of the Persian Gulf. Anyway, he assures us, if foreigners make a trifle using home-brewed red wine, jelly and packet custard, with hundreds and thousands to decorate the top, the Kuwaitis love it.

Even further south, the southern end of the Red Sea, we find a multi-coloured curiosity in the form of a dessert confection which resembles an English trifle but exhibits the colours of the Italian flag and has the Italian name *Zuppa Inglese*, suggesting that it could have been introduced to the country during the period of Italian occupation. The recipe is given in a charming book on *Taste of Eritrea* by the American author Olivia Warren, who worked there for some years, taking note of local foodstuffs and cookery.

Her recipe, which follows the numbered sequence pattern favoured by some authors on both sides of the Atlantic, calls for two kinds of pudding mix, vanilla and pistachio. These are not available everywhere, but we found that by making a quantity of custard and flavouring half of it with vanilla and the other half with pistachio, the result was satisfactorily to the original specification. The main thing to remember is that the custard will have to set and that the colour scheme (pale cream, green and the red provided by the grenadine syrup for the third layer) should be fully apparent.

ERITREAN TRIFLE
(*Zuppa Inglese*)

12 ladyfingers; ½ cup rum or peach brandy; 1 (3.9 ounce) package vanilla pudding mix; 5 ⅔ cups half-and-half [whipping cream] (about 3 pints); ½ teaspoon vanilla extract; 2 cups fresh raspberries or 2 cups of sliced bananas; 1 (3.9 ounce) package pistachio pudding mix; ¼ cup crushed unsalted pistachios; ⅓ cup grenadine; ⅛ teaspoon salt; 2 tablespoons cornstarch; 2 cups whipping cream; ¼ cup slivered almonds.

1. Moisten the ladyfingers with the rum. Arrange them against the inside of the bowl, leaving spaces between them.

2. Prepare the vanilla pudding according to package inst-ructions, but substitute 2 cups of half-and-half in place of milk, and add ½ tsp vanilla extract.

3. Fill the bottom third of the bowl with the vanilla pudding.

4. Arrange 1 cup of the raspberries on top of the vanilla pudding.

5. Prepare the pistachio pudding according to package instructions, but substitute 2 cups of half-and-half in place of milk and stir in the pistachios.

6. Fill the middle third of the bowl with pistachio pudding, and arrange the remaining cup of raspberries on top of it.

7. Make pomegranate pudding by whisking together the grenadine, the remaining 1 ⅔ cups of half-and-half, salt, and cornstarch. Heat it over a low heat while stirring constantly for 8 minutes, until it comes to a boil and thickens.

8. Fill the top third of the bowl with the pomegranate pudding to within an inch of the top. Place the bowl in the refrigerator to chill for 3 hours.

9. Whip the cream until it forms stiff peaks and pile it above the top of the bowl. Sprinkle the whipped cream with the almond slivers and serve.

We had not realized that there is a Zulu aspect to the history of trifles until we mentioned our interest to Peter James-Smith in South Africa, and received from him the following fascinating report.

A bit of information about Trifles that may be of use. Blacks generally have little interest in desserts other than the Zulus who have a great love of English Trifle! Trifle has always been a South African favourite and at about the end of the nineteenth century a regional difference appeared in the form of the addition of preserved fruits such as green figs above the sponge cake layer.

The reference is in Peter Veldsman's *The Flavours of South Africa* (published by Tafelberg 1998), under his introduction to Desserts. I spoke to Peter about it as to his source of information and he said that it came from a Zulu who was not quite westernized. We discussed the ingredients which would naturally be sponge cake, jelly and tinned fruit with an "Ultramel" topping. Ultramel is a pre-prepared custard that comes in a carton like a milk carton. If not that it would be condensed milk, whipped.

At lunchtime today I sat next to a friend of mine, Dorah Sithole, who is the food editor of *True Love Magazine* – a family magazine for the Black Market. She has a number of books on African food to her credit, the latest being *Cape to Cairo* which I find very useful for reference purposes, and she confirmed what Peter Veldsman had to say.

Peter James-Smith also indicated that he could provide a trifle recipe of 1918 from the Eastern Cape, but he doubted 'whether you could stand up after eating it', since it included a whole half tumbler of brandy and sherry mixed. In fact it seems that there was a tendency in South Africa to use a lot of liquor (unless antipodean tumblers were unusually small). Consider the amounts in the recipe which we finally chose to represent the settlers in South Africa, and which is reproduced below. It comes from the charming and decorous book *Hilda's "Where Is it"? of Recipes* by Hildagonda J. Duckitt (1891, but our copy is of the revised edition, 1895, complete with all the blank pages for notes and the slim pencil in its attached holder). Since this item is excessively rare and has not been fully described in the best available bibliography (Driver, 1989, who mentions only the presence of a pencil in a later edition, of 1911, and without a description of the pencil), we mention here that the slim pencil bears the inscription 'Perry & Co's patent "WEE JOHN BULL" (Germany)' and measures 152 mm in length. The finish is a very dark brown, glossy and with the handle end decorated in silver, more or less matching the lettering.

TRIFLE.
(Mrs. Etheridge's Book.)

INGREDIENTS
1 tumbler of Madeira or Sherry.
a wineglass of French Brandy.
4 Sponge Biscuits.
½ lb. of Macaroons.
1 pint of rich Boiled Custard.
1 pint of Syllabub.

Soak four sponge biscuits and half a pound of macaroons in the Madeira and French brandy. Then cover the bottom of a glass dish with half of these, pour over them a pint of rich custard previously made, then lay the remainder of the soaked biscuits upon them, and pile over the whole, to the depth of two or three inches, the whipped syllabub, well drained; the whipped syllabub to be made the day before, or some hours, before, as follows: Take half a pint of cream, half a glass of light wine, and a dessertspoonful of sifted sugar; take a clean dry whisk, and whip the cream to a stiff froth with the wine, adding the sugar last of all. When the wine has drained to the bottom, carefully skim the light, frothy cream, and pack it on the top of the last layer of macaroons. *Excellent.*

CHAPTER EIGHT

TRIFLING RELATIONS

An author writing about relations of the trifle in, say, 1700 would have come up with a list very different from ours, including for example white pot and fool (for both of which see the Glossary). He would have said nothing about the trifling relations which we list, since these were not heard of until after the introduction of the 'modern' trifle in the 1750s.

There would have been one item common to a 1700 list and to ours of 2000. This is the syllabub, which has appeared since 1751, and still appears nowadays, as the topping of certain trifles, but which in olden times was usually a free-standing item. For earlier syllabub recipes one cannot do better than read the magnificent essay by Ivan Day, 'Further Musings on Syllabub', in *PPC* 53 (1996). This distinguishes between no fewer than nine categories of old recipes for syllabub. (See also the Glossary.) Some readers, content to skip the research and eager to find a recipe they can easily use, will find such recipes on pages 34 and 61–62; and two interesting and innovative recipes, created in the latter part of the twentieth century, one on page 57 and the other at the end of this chapter.

As for the relations of the modern trifle, we have already paid sufficient attention to one or two (e.g. Floating Island on page 19 and see also the Glossary) and have provided trailers for some of the more exotic relations, such as the tribe of tipsy squires etc. referred to in Chapter Six. Here our purpose is to list what we perceive as the main trifling relations of modern (post 1750) times and to provide at least illustrative recipe for each of the categories which we discern.

Whim-whams

This is another, and amusing, name given for a trifle in the eighteenth century. It is described in the *OED*, in fact the entry for it is highly recommended reading. The main definition is, 'A fanciful or fantastic object; fig. a trifle; in early use chiefly, a trifling ornament of dress, a trinket; later in various local uses.' A reference to 'Whimwhams & whirligiggs to please Baboones' is startling as is the question posed by a character in (1602) 'Dost loue that mother Mumble crust, dost thou? dost long for that whim-wham?' Fiona Lucraft writing in *PPC* 57 (1997) was even more struck by a little verse in Skelton (1529) which seems to be describing a lady's hat:

> After the Sarasyns gyse,
> With a whym wham,
> Knyt with a trym tram,
> Vpon her brayne pan.

The whim-wham recipes we have chosen are, first, one from Hannah Glasse's *The Compleat Confectioner* (*c.* 1760) and, secondly, the recipe given by the Scottish author Mrs Dalgairns (*Practice of Cookery*, 2nd edn., 1829).

A whim-wham

Take a pint of sack and ½ pound of Naples biscuit. Put them in a deep dish or bowl and let them stand for 10 minutes. Take a quart of cream. Whisk it well. Pour over the wine and biscuits. Send it to the table directly. It must be made just as you are going to use it.

You must mind to use just enough biscuit to soak up the wine, no more.

And Mrs Dalgairns' recipe:

Whim Wham.

Sweeten a quart of cream and mix with it a tea-cupful of white wine, and the grated peel of a lemon; whisk it to a froth, which drain upon the back of a sieve, and put part into a deep glass dish; cut some Naples biscuit as thin as possible, and put a layer lightly over the froth, and one of red currant jelly, then a layer of the froth, and one of the biscuit and jelly; finish with the froth, and pour the remainder of the cream into the dish and garnish with citron and candied orange peel cut into straws.

Tipsy cakes are sponge cakes or victoria sandwich cakes which are soaked with, typically, sherry or other wine and decorated with cream. Popular since the late eighteenth century, they are clearly related to trifles, yet forming a distinct category which in turn merges into the category of tipsy puddings.

John Ayto, as so often, tells us when the term reportedly first appeared in print: Mary Russell Mitford wrote in 1806 that 'We had tipsy cake on one side, and grape tart on the other.'

However the earliest recipe we have selected is a little later: it comes from Meg Dods (1829):

> *Tipsy Cake.* – Crumble a fresh-baked pound sponge-cake into a trifle-dish. Pour over it as much wine, with one-fourth brandy, as it will imbibe, and heap on it whipt cream seasoned as for trifle.

Our next recipe is from Eliza Acton's *Modern Cookery* (1860) who also gives it the alternative name of Brandy Trifle.

Tipsy Cake, or Brandy Trifle

> The old-fashioned mode of preparing this dish was to soak a light sponge or Savoy cake in as much good French brandy as it could absorb; then, to stick it full of blanched almonds cut into whole-length spikes, and to pour a rich cold boiled custard round it. It is more usual now to pour white wine over the cake, or a mixture of wine and brandy; with this the juice of half a lemon is sometimes mixed.

Other names and versions exist in other countries such as tipsy laird, parson or squire (especially in America); for some of these see page 99.

An interesting variation on the tipsy cake theme is provided by Florence White (1932), who proposes a 'hedgehog tipsy cake'.

The hedgehog is a pudding which enjoyed some popularity in England in the eighteenth and nineteenth centuries. It was so called because of the flaked almonds which were stuck into its upper surface, where they resembled spines. Three early examples, with the hedgehogs made of marzipan, are in Hannah Glasse's *Art of Cookery Made Plain and Easy* (1747). Perhaps that was the time when hedgehogs suddenly came into fashion. This would support the claim made by Florence White in *Good Things in England* (1932) that her extraordinary recipe for 'Hedgehog Tipsy Cake' originated in the eighteenth century, although it reached her through 'Gladys Langley, Acton, 1931'. As she gives it, it is an extreme example of the cookery by numbers school of recipe writing, so in the version below we give a less staccato paraphrase, while preserving step number 10 in her own prose.

Hedgehog Tipsy Cake

The ingredients are:

A stale oval-shaped sponge or Madeira cake;
fruit syrup, or wine to soak;
apricot jam 2 tablespoonfuls;
grated chocolate a tablespoonful;
raisins 2 for the eyes; sweet almonds 3 oz;
orange (or lemon) juice ¼ pint; castor sugar 3 oz;
cream ½ pint; red currant jelly 2 tablespoonfuls.

The author explains that, on the day before this sweet is required, the cake is cut to represent the body of a hedgehog, fining off one end to represent the head and nose. Then place the hedgehog in the dish in which it is to be served, scoop a cup-shaped piece out of the middle of the back, fill the hollow thus made with wine or syrup, let it soak well in, replace the cut out piece in the hollow, but keep on pouring liquid over the cake, which must be soaked through and through.

On the next day stick in two raisins for his eyes. Blanch the almonds, split them lengthwise, in three or four thin strips, and brown them in the oven. Two of these are to form 'eyebrows' above the raisin eyes. The others are to be stuck into the cake 'beginning at the back and sloping them backwards so as to present a fine backward sweep when the whole back and sides are covered'.

To prepare for the final step, put the orange (or lemon) juice in a basin with the sugar. Then …

'10. Add the half pint of fresh cream and whisk until very thick; this is a SOLID SILLABUB, and should be piled in the dish round the hedgehog. Finish by putting some red currant jelly just in front of the hedgehog to look as if he is eating it.'

On the left, a Tipsy Cake, based on an illustration in Mrs Beeton, 1861; on the right a Hedgehog Tipsy Cake, drawn by Soun.

TIPSY PARSONS AND TIPSY SQUIRES

Since Florence White's original unknown source of the eighteenth century has taken Tipsy cake into the animal world, it is but a short step to human beings, which perhaps accounts for the wide range of people whose names are given to certain of these cakes. Parsons, squires, lairds, etc. – what do they have in common? Nothing, it would seem, except for being tipsy and probably living in a rural environment, often in North America.

Mention has already been made on page 39 of the recipe to which Elizabeth Craig gave the name 'Old-Fashioned Tipsy Kent Squire'. It is unusual for tipsy animals or human beings to be given a geographical location; indeed this may be the only instance.

One would expect to find a difference between things called cakes and things called puddings, but a study of numerous examples suggests that whether a confection was called Tipsy cake or Tipsy cake pudding or Tipsy pudding depended simply on the preference of the author. Nonetheless, Tipsy cake puddings look like a different genre, so we give one example, from Lucy Jones, *Puddings and Sweets* (1877).

Tipsy Cake Pudding

Take six penny sponge-cakes and cut them in half long ways; place raspberry or any other preserve between, and lay them in rather a deep dish; pour over them a wine-glassful of brandy and water (equal parts). Then make a custard with the yolks of three eggs and rather more than half a pint of milk sweetened and flavoured to taste; pour it over the cakes. With a whisk beat up the whites of the eggs to a strong froth, and pour lightly on the top of all.

We wish to mention items from *The Comprehensive Pudding Book* (*c.* 1875) because the three puddings given there bear titles in French as well as English, which produces a pleasantly quaint effect. Tipsy Pudding à la Savoy is 'Pouding à l'Ivrogne à la Savoie'. And we note in the Tipsy pudding recipe given by 'Wyvern' (Colonel A.R. Kenney-Herbert, see Bibliography) in 1885 that his dish inspired him to introduce the seventeenth-century verb 'tipsify' (make someone tipsy) into a culinary context. Here is his recipe.

TIPSY PUDDING

Cut up a stale Madeira cake into slices, and with them line the bottom of a large glass dish, tipsify them with wine, or any nice liqueur and spread a layer of any good jam over them, or one of preserved fruit like cherries, peaches, or apricots.

Make a rich custard, and add to it an ounce of dissolved gelatine. When cold, set the dish on ice and pour a very little of the custard round the cake and fruit, letting it set by degrees. When at length the cake, etc., is firmly congealed in custard, complete its covering with the rest thereof, and let it consolidate. Garnish the surfce with whipped cream, and serve straight from the ice.

WASSAIL BOWL

Meg Dods (1829) explains that 'This is, in fact, just a rich eating posset, or the more modern *Tipsy-Cake* ... .' In a pleasant touch she adds that: 'The wassail-bowl was anciently crowned with garlands and ribbons, and ushered in the carols and songs, – a custom worthy of revival.'

Wassail-bowl, a centre Supper Dish for Christmas-tide. – Crumble down as for trifle a fresh rice-cake (or use macaroons or other small biscuit) into a china punch-bowl or deep glass dish. Over this pour some sweet, rich wine, as Malmsey Madeira, if wanted very rich, but raisin-wine will do. Sweeten this, and pour a high-seasoned rich custard over it. Strew nutmeg and grated sugar lightly over it, and ornament it with sliced blanched almonds.

SWISS CREAM AND DEAN'S CREAM

Confections resembling, in varying degrees, conventional trifles have sometimes been referred to as 'creams'. Of our two examples, 'Swiss Cream' is defined by the *OED* as a kind of trifle, and seems to have enjoyed a limited vogue in the nineteenth century, appearing in Eliza Acton (*c.* 1860), in the version given overleaf, and also in Mrs Beeton (1861) and Garrett (*c.* 1895). By the way, a main characteristic of anything called Swiss Cream seems to be the presence of lemon and/or lemon rind; the latter appears in the very first line of Eliza Acton's recipe.

SWISS CREAM, OR TRIFLE
(*Very Good*)

Flavour pleasantly with lemon rind and cinnamon, a pint of rich cream, after having taken from it as much as will mix smoothly to a thin batter four teaspoonsful of the finest flour; sweeten it with six ounces of well-refined sugar in lumps; place it over a clear fire in a delicately clean saucepan, and when it boils stir in the flour, and simmer it for four or five minutes, stirring it gently without ceasing; then pour it out, and when it is quite cold mix with it by degrees the strained juice of two moderate-sized and very fresh lemons. Take a quarter of a pound of macaroons, cover the bottom of a glass dish with a portion of them, pour in a part of the cream, lay the remainder of the macaroons upon it, add the rest of the cream, and ornament it with candied citron sliced thin. It should be made the day before it is wanted for table. The requisite flavour may be given to the dish by infusing in the cream the very thin rind of a lemon and part of a stick of cinnamon slightly bruised, and then straining it before the flour is added; or, these and the sugar may be boiled together with two or three spoonsful of water, to a strongly flavoured syrup, which, after having been passed through a muslin strainer, may be stirred into the cream. Some cooks boil the cinnamon and the *grated* rind of a lemon with all the other ingredients, but the cream has then to be pressed through a sieve after it is made, a process which it is always desirable to avoid. It may be flavoured with vanilla and maraschino, or with orange blossoms at pleasure; but is *excellent* made as above.

Rich cream, 1 pint; sugar, 6 oz; rind, 1 lemon; cinnamon, 1 drachm; flour, 4 teaspoonsful; juice, 2 lemons; macaroons, 4 oz.; candied citron, 1 to 2 oz.

Florence White, introducing a recipe for 'Dean's Cream' in *Good Things in England* (1932), said that it was 'another favourite Cambridge pudding, an eighteenth-century recipe used up to the time of the Great War'. We have not been able to find an eighteenth-century source, and surmise that the recipe may originally have appeared in a manuscript recipe book. The Cambridge connection no doubt reflects the interest in puddings which Cambridge colleges have been showing for centuries; cf Trinity College and Burnt Cream.

THE DEAN'S CREAM

INGREDIENTS: sponge cakes; raspberry jam; orange marmalade; ratafias; sherry; brandy; cream ¾ pint; glacé cherries; pineapple; angelica

METHOD:

1. Spread some sponge cakes with raspberry jam.
2. And some with orange or apricot marmalade; arrange them in a dish alternately.
3. Add some ratafias.
4. Soak the cake with sherry.
5. Sweeten ¾ pint of cream, add a wineglassful brandy, whip till very very thick, and
6. Pour over the soaked cake; decorate with cherries, pineapple and angelica.

[NOTE: Helen found that this worked well with 8 small fairy cakes, 16 small macaroons, and about 200 ml of sweet sherry.]

And finally here is a modern version of the syllabub which has been given to us by Chris Payne, who in turn got it from the magazine *Supercook*, a series which flourished in the 1970s. We have adapted it very slightly. It demonstrates the sort of variations which are possible. We found the combination of the grape and ginger flavours particularly refreshing.

White Grape and Ginger Syllabub
(to serve 8–10)

1 kg seedless white grapes
250 g crushed ginger biscuits
4 egg whites, stiffly beaten
250 g castor sugar
300 ml white wine
Juice of half a lemon
450 ml of double cream
50 g toasted flaked almonds

Arrange one quarter of the grapes on the bottom of a medium-sized serving bowl. Cover with one quarter of the biscuit crumbs. Continue making layers until the grapes and the crumbs are used up.

Set aside.

Place the beaten egg whites in a medium sized mixing bowl and beat in one quarter of the sugar. Fold in the remaining sugar and then pour over the wine and lemon juice and stir everything carefully until they are thoroughly combined.

Set aside.

Pour the cream into a large mixing bowl and beat until it is thick but not stiff. Fold the egg mixture into the cream and then pour the cream mixture over the fruit and biscuit mix.

Place in the fridge to chill for 2 hours.

Sprinkle with almonds before serving.

CHAPTER NINE

ITALY: ZUPPA INGLESE AND TIRAMISU

Zuppa Inglese 'is an Italian dessert which is related in composition (sponge cake/biscuits, liqueur, custard and/or cream, optional topping/decoration), although not necessarily in ancestry, to the English trifle.' This explanation and most of what follows is taken from *The Oxford Companion to Food* (2nd impression, 2000).

At first glance the name would seem to mean 'English soup'. In fact, *zuppa* and the French term *soupe* and the English word 'sop' referred in medieval times to pieces of bread set to soak in broth. Then with the passage of time the mixture of bread and broth took on the name (which now became 'soup' in English). Eventually the primary meaning of the terms in the three languages became soup, as the word is now used, whether or not pieces of bread are present. Yet the old meaning lingered on in certain expressions, including Italian use of *zuppa* for a sweet confection with a cake-like or biscuit basis. There are quite a few of these confections, the *inglese* version being only one.

Explanations of *inglese* vary. An attractive one is that of Fernanda Gosetti (1993), which reads thus in translation:

> This is a classic dessert of Siena, known there as *zuppa del duca* and at Florence as *zuppa inglese*. One of my dearest Sienese friends told me that the dessert had a very ancient origin. It was served in 1552 on the occasion of a banquet offered by the Duke of Correggio (whence the name *del duca*) who had been invited to go to Siena by Cosimo de Medici to help the Sienese by finding a peaceful solution to a dispute between them and the Spaniards. After the banquet, the Duke was convinced that the Sienese had no need of help. Once back in Florence, the Duke introduced the dessert to the Medici court, where it found enormous favour, especially among the English, who at that time were

numerous in Florence; so much so that the dessert became known under the name *zuppa degli inglesi*, or more simply, *zuppa inglese*.

If this explanation is correct, it seems that the use of the name *zuppa inglese* in its familiar sense must have supplanted, in the sixteenth century, an earlier meaning. Sabban and Serventi (1995), to whom much of the information presented here is due, point out that Cristoforo di Messisbugo (1557) gave a recipe entitled *A fare una suppa magra inglese* which was for something quite different; it involved making a bouillon of parsley roots, to be bound with egg yolk and verjuice and poured over slices of bread, the whole being served with a powdering of sugar and cinnamon. No earlier reference to *suppa (zuppa) inglese* has been traced. Nor, apparently, is it known when the name was first applied to the dessert. But it does seem clear that the dessert had its origin in Italy and should not be regarded as a derivative of English trifle. It is, however, hard to determine whether it belongs originally to Piedmont (as the authoritative dictionary of Piedmontese food terms by Doglio, 1995, claims) or to Tuscany or Naples, as others believe.

The alcoholic ingredients for the dessert would normally be rum, Marsala or the liqueur called Alchermes, which imparts a fine red colour (see Glossary); this is not easy to find in England – the bottle we eventually located was in Edinburgh.

For Zuppa Inglese ordinary sponge cake or sponge biscuits may be used but Italians would probably choose *pan di Spagna* (meaning 'Spanish bread') or Savoiardi biscuits.

Many variations may be found in parts of central and southern Italy. In the south, the zuppa may have a meringue topping. In Emilia-Romagna it may have layers of two different custards: egg custard and chocolate custard. In Tuscany, the zuppa is often more liquid than elsewhere.

For a representative recipe, to be chosen from the scores available, we have recourse to John Mariani, a connoisseur of Italian food both in Italy and in the USA, and the author of *The Dictionary of Italian Food and Drink*, 1998. The recipe comes from this book.

Zuppa Inglese
(to serve 6)

4 cups milk
8 eggs, separated
1 cup confectioners' sugar
¼ cup flour
½ vanilla bean
1 sponge cake
1 cup rum
½ cup Alchermes

Warm the milk in a saucepan but do not bring to a boil. In a bowl, beat the egg yolks, ⅔ cup of the sugar, the flour, and vanilla and gradually pour into heated milk. Keep mixing with a wooden spoon until thickened to a custard-like consistency. Remove the vanilla bean.

Cut the sponge cake horizontally into 3 layers. Take 1 layer and place it in a deep serving dish. Sprinkle with half the rum and some of the Alchermes. Spread half the custard onto the cake. Cut up the next layer of sponge cake into pieces about 1 inch long and ½ inch thick. Place on top of the custard, sprinkle with the rest of the rum and Alchermes, and spread the remaining custard on top. Cover with the third layer of sponge cake.

Whip the egg whites until they form soft peaks and combine with the remaining sugar. Cover the cake with the whipped egg whites and brown under the broiler. Allow to cool and chill in the refrigerator until ready to serve.

This recipe has been given to us by Jack Conte; it is for the Zuppa Inglese his mother likes to make in summer in Sicily, an island renowned for the striking appearance of its desserts and confectionery. Serves 6–8.

10–12 Savoiardi biscuits
(or thin slices of pan di Spagna)
50 ml Marsala all'uovo
400 ml orange jelly (see below)
3 ripe peaches, peeled and cut in sections
1 small bunch seedless white grapes, halved
1 slice water melon, seeds removed and cut in small cubes
5 drops vanilla essence
300 g whipping cream
1½ tbs icing sugar
100 g mascarpone cheese
a few strawberries or extra grapes for decoration

Use a bowl, preferably crystal, about 10 cm deep and 25 cm in diameter. Place the Savoiardi biscuits in the bottom and soak them with the Marsala. Next place the peaches, grapes and water melon on top.

Make the orange jelly with leaf gelatin as required, the juice of 1 orange and 1 tbs sugar, aiming at a firm consistency (not runny). Pour over the fruit and place the bowl in the refrigerator and leave to set. (Ideally this should be done the day before the Zuppa Inglese is needed.)

Whip the cream lightly. Mix in the icing sugar, the mascarpone cheese and the vanilla. Stir well to combine the ingredients.

Cover the fruit in the bowl with the cream mixture, spreading it flat with a knife, reserving some to be used as decoration.

Now decorate with the strawberries and grapes and pipe the remaining cream on top.

Tirami Sù

This rich Italian dessert is now familiar to many people in the English speaking world. Our recipe, to serve 8, comes from Jane Grigson's *The Cooking of the Mediterranean* (1991).

Tirami Sù 'Whip-me-up'

'The engaging name of this Italian pudding groups it with fools, trifles, whim-whams – in other words you can whip it up in a few minutes, it's nothing, a trifle, any fool can do it. ...'

1 fatless sponge cake
270 ml black coffee made from medium roast beans and lightly
*   sweetened*
sugar

FOR THE FILLING:
400 g mascarpone or full-fat soft cheese
4 large egg yolks
100 g caster sugar
2 tbs rum or brandy
2 large egg whites (optional)
50–75 g bitter or plain chocolate, grated

Make the filling first. Beat the mascarpone or soft cheese until it is very smooth. Then whisk the egg yolks and sugar to a billowing yellow mass, either electrically, or with a whisk and copper bowl over very hot water. Remove the bowl from the heat and allow to cool slightly. Fold the mascarpone into the cooled egg mixture, with the alcohol. If you want to lighten the cream, whisk the whites until they are stiff and fold them in gently.

Slice the cake across into 3 or 4 layers. Dip the upper side of the bottom layer into the lightly sweetened coffee, and put it coffee side up on a plate. Spread with the mascarpone cream and scatter with chocolate. Repeat with the other layers, finishing with mascarpone evenly scattered with chocolate. Chill for at least an hour before serving.

The following description of tirami sù by Anna del Conte (1987) includes an indication of its origin and a reference to its growing international popularity – still growing at such a speed that it will soon be almost ubiquitous, at least in restaurants.

> This dessert, which was created about twenty years ago [i.e. in the 1960s] by the owner of the El Toulá restaurant of Treviso, is already a favorite in many countries outside Italy.
>
> Tiramisu means "pick-me-up," which the dessert does as it is generously laced with brandy. There are several versions made with pan di Spagna or Savoiardi soaked with brandy and Espresso coffee, layered with a mascarpone and egg cream, flavored with chocolate.

Tirami sù has spread much further and more widely than Zuppa Inglese, but the latter or something like it can be found in various places where Italian influence has been strong. Thus there is a group of recipes in Albania which Maria Kaneva-Johnson in her book *The Melting Pot, Balkan Food and Cookery* (1995) describes as 'Albanian Trifle Creams'. The Albanian name is *Zupa*, from the Italian Zuppa Inglese. Maria's own favourite recipe uses two kinds of custard, plain chocolate and chopped green pistachio nuts, among other items. She states that there as many Albanian recipes for *Zupa* as there are English ones for trifle, which suggests that this Italian dessert has grown very strong roots on the other side of the Adriatic.

In this connection see also the Eritrean trifle at page 90. And it is possible to discern echoes of Zuppa Inglese in the Maltese trifle which is strangely named 'Soufflé' (see the chapter on Oddities, page 116).

CHAPTER TEN

ODDITIES

There can be no doubt about savoury trifles being oddities. So we start this chapter with two of them.

We met Theodore Francis Garrett and his monumental *Encyclopaedia of Practical Cookery* (c. 1895) on page 36, and reproduced his Queen of Trifles, a regal dessert. Here we offer one of his two savoury trifles.

Cold Savoury Trifle

Cut a slice about 1 in thick off a stale loaf, trim it to a square shape, removing all the crust, and make a hollow in the centre. Put a large piece of lard in a frying-pan, and when it boils, put in the bread, and fry it a pale golden brown. Then put it on a sieve to drain. Roughly chop the flesh of a lobster; prepare a nice fresh salad, and place it in a dish. Fill the hollow of the croustade with the lobster, put it in the centre of the salad, and pour over a nicely-flavoured mayonnaise sauce. Ornament the dish prettily with various shapes cut out of whites of hard-boiled eggs, carrots, and beetroot, and serve.

If a cold savoury trifle is odd, a hot savoury trifle must be counted odder still. The following recipe for such a surprising item comes from *The "Pudding Lady's" Recipe Book* by Florence Petty (1917).

BEEF TRIFLE.

1 lb cold meat, chopped finely; 1 tablespoon horseradish, grated; 3 oz breadcrumbs; ½ onion, chopped; 2 oz margarine; 1 egg; pepper and salt to taste

Mix well together. Place in small cups, greased. Bake in moderate oven 20 minutes. Turn out and serve on a hot dish with gravy round.

The name of Afghanistan's capital city would not normally conjure up thoughts or visions of trifles, nor would the city of Vientiane in Laos. However, trifles can be conjured up in any part of the world by those who have an inventive spirit and are prepared to apply the English concept of a trifle to ingredients from elsewhere.

Firstly, Helen writes: this recipe has been inspired by my Afghan husband, who asked me to devise a trifle recipe with an eastern flavour, and to name it after the city in which he was born and brought up. The second reason for including this recipe is that the results are really good. An alternative to the yoghurt topping could be an Afghan *firni*, a sort of custard made with milk and cornflour flavoured with rosewater and cardamon. There is a recipe for this in my book *Noshe Djan – Afghan Food and Cookery*.

KABUL QUINCE AND YOGHURT TRIFLE

2 medium quinces
110 g sugar
juice of ½ lemon
pinch of ground cardamom
18–24 amaretti biscuits
500 g Greek strained yoghurt
¼ tsp saffron
1 tbs rose water
110 g caster sugar
½ tsp ground cardamom
toasted flaked almonds
slivered or ground pistachio
crystallized rose petals (optional)

Peel, core and slice the quinces thinly. Put into a pan and add water, which should well cover the quinces. Bring to the boil, cover with a lid, turn down the heat and simmer until they are just soft. (You may have to add more water if it reduces too much.) Remove the quinces with a slotted spoon from the pan and set to one side.

Now add the sugar to the water in which the quinces were cooked and stir to dissolve. Add the lemon juice. Bring to the boil and cook for a couple of minutes until syrupy. Remove from the heat, add the cardamom and return the quinces to the pan. Leave to cool in the syrup.

Place the amaretti biscuits in the bottom of a glass bowl and cover with the quinces. Add just enough of the syrup to lightly soak the amaretti.

Now make the yoghurt cream. Dissolve the saffron in the rosewater and beat into the yoghurt. Mix in the sugar, more or less according to taste, and add the cardamom. Mix well.

Spread the yoghurt cream evenly over the quinces and decorate with the almonds and pistachios and rose petals, according to your fancy.

Vientiane Coconut Jelly Trifle

Alan's recipe is inspired directly by his experience of living in Laos and exploring the *Traditional Dishes of Laos* (the title of an extraordinary book on the subject by Phia Sing) including several desserts which have evolved there on the basis of the coconut, most versatile of foodstuffs. It is accompanied by one of only a large number of potential variations. Marry the English trifle to an Asian cuisine and you will be astonished by the number of progeny which this coupling produces.

The ingredients include first and second extractions of coconut milk. To produce these you would need one large or two smaller fresh ripe coconuts and a knowledge of the technique. It is easier for most people to use desiccated coconut, following the instructions on the packet to produce the right amount.

In the recipe which follows, since the versatile coconut can also be used to produce coconut custard, you could substitute this for the tapioca. This would be made with, for example, 4 eggs (lightly beaten), half a cup of sugar and a cup of thick coconut milk. Set over a low heat and stir frequently until you have a custard consistency.

STAGE ONE – THE JELLY

2 heaped tsp agar agar (in powdered form)
170 ml thick coconut milk (first extraction)
670 ml thin coconut milk (second extraction)
salt, to taste
70 g brown sugar
70 g white sugar
2 eggs, lightly beaten

Add the agar agar to the thick coconut milk in a cooking pot, stir and bring to the boil. Add salt and both kinds of sugar and leave to simmer for nearly ten minutes. Then add the thin coconut milk to the mixture.

Have your trifle dish, which should be heat-proof, ready. Pour the beaten eggs into the bottom of it.

Bring the coconut mixture back to the boil, then pour it quickly over the beaten eggs and leave to set. (The result, which has settled into a jelly of two layers, the upper one brown and the lower one much paler, can be served by itself as the Lao dessert called *Vun*, but we are going on to add further layers.)

STAGE TWO – FRUIT AND TAPIOCA

My idea here need not be spelled out in detail, because choice of fruits, quantity of tapioca etc. are all flexible. However, I would suggest making at least two cups of tapioca pudding (I would use 'Minute' tapioca, and follow the directions on the packet) and then setting it aside to cool.

Meanwhile you could thinly slice a banana or two, sprinkle with lime juice, and lay over the *vun*. Then add a layer of the now cool tapioca, and top with thin pieces of peeled mango, either simple strips or (fancier) crescent shapes, making a decorative pattern. Very thin slices of pineapple would be an alternative topping.

Next we come to something which is not a trifle but by a piece of unparalleled impertinence bears the name. This is followed by something which is a trifle but does not bear the name.

Ann Semple writes: 'Peg Bracken was a woman who made a career in the 1960s of doing as little in and about the house as possible. Her first book, *The I Hate To Cook Book,* was published in 1960 and was, as I recall, a runaway success. It was quickly followed by several other volumes, all delightful to read and often to emulate: *The I Hate to Housekeep Book,* (1962); *I Try to Behave Myself; The I Hate to Cook Almanack (A Book of Days);* and *Appendix to The I Hate to Cook Book* among others. Of the volumes listed, I now possess every one, including the *Appendix* in which I found Peg Bracken's take on trifle.' Her recipe follows:

London Trifle
[Note breath-taking simplicity here]

1 cup yogurt
1 cup marmalade

Mix them up. Then taste. Maybe you'll want more yogurt. Or marmalade. Spoon it into sherbet glasses, grate some orange rind on top, and chill it a bit.

[NOTE BY ALAN: In testing this concoction I decided to simplify it further by omitting the sherbet glasses, the grated orange rind and the whole tedious business of chilling. Just leave it all in the bowl (and save on the washing up).]

As an antidote to Peg Bracken's perversely exaggerated simplicity, we show a drawing adapted from Garrett (c. 1895) which represents the other end of the simple/complex spectrum.

Anne and Helen Caruana Galizia are co-authors of an admirable book on *The Food & Cookery of Malta*, which bears many a mark of scholarship as well as practical experience in Maltese kitchens. However, the name of this recipe in their book, which as they point out bears no resemblance to classic French hot or cold soufflés, defeated their scholarly enquiries. It seems that no-one has an explanation. But, plainly, we have here a trifle.

MALTESE TRIFLE
Soufflé

375 ml home-made egg custard (some of it may be chocolate flavoured); 6 large slices of sponge cake; 2–3 tbs apricot or strawberry jam; 125 ml brandy, sherry or rum; 300 g rikotta; 3 tbs caster sugar; 50 g dark chocolate, chopped; 50 g candied peel.

TO FINISH: 2 egg whites; 50 g caster sugar; bitter chocolate, chopped almonds, roasted, chopped.

Use a large glass bowl. Pour in a layer of custard. Slice the sponge cake and spread with jam. Arrange a layer over the custard. Sprinkle with brandy, sherry or rum. Beat the lumps out of the *rikotta* and mix with the caster sugar, chocolate and candied peel. Lay a layer of this on the sponge cake. Repeat the process, continuing until all the ingredients have been used up. Finish with a layer of custard.

Whisk the egg whites until stiff. Whisk in the caster sugar. Spoon over the trifle, decorating with more chopped chocolate and some chopped roasted almonds. Clearly the meringue topping must have evolved in the absence of cream.

Since there are still some people in the world who cling to the belief that there are such things as aphrodisiac foods, and since these people might be disappointed if they found that there was nothing relevant to their pet subject in the present book, we conclude it with an item which, sort of, caters to this requirement. We had been intrigued by a recipe for 'White Chocolate Strawberry Trifle' in *Inter Courses: an aphrodisiac cookbook* by Martha Hopkins and Randall

Lockridge (1997) and decided to create our own version. It is a really good trifle. But, no more aphrodisiac quality can be detected in it than in the hundreds and thousands of other foods and dishes which have been hopefully put forward to play the role of the crock of gold at the rainbow's end. The recipe is for 2 people.

APHRODISIAC TRIFLE

25 g caster sugar / 1 egg yolk
50 g mascarpone cheese
50 ml whipping cream
½ tsp vanilla essence
6–8 medium-sized strawberries
50 ml black coffee, flavoured with ½ tbs brandy
4 boudoir biscuits
25 g grated white chocolate
crystallized rose petals
Biscuits Roses de Reims (optional)

Beat well the sugar and egg yolk together. Add the mascarpone and beat until smooth. Whisk the whipping cream until stiff, then blend it and the vanilla into the mascarpone mixture and chill.

Slice the strawberries, reserving two whole for decoration.

Break the boudoir biscuits into 4 pieces. Dip the pieces in the coffee and distribute them evenly into two individual sundae glasses. Over each, add in turn layers of chocolate, sliced strawberry and mascarpone mixture. Top each with a whole strawberry and decorate with the rose petals.

Serve with the lovely pink Biscuits Roses de Reims, if desired.

GLOSSARY OF TRIFLING TERMS

ACITRÓN, the candied stem of the large cushion-like biznaga cactus, *Echninocactus grandis*, is sometimes called just *biznaga* in Mexico, where it is made. It is usually shaped into bars of about 2 cm square, and mainly used for desserts. In the USA it goes under the name of 'cactus candy'. CANDIED CITRON can be substituted; indeed, this has always been what the term *acitrón* has meant in Spain.

ALCHERMES (or ALKERMÈS) is a sweet, crimson-coloured liqueur made from rose petals, iris, jasmine and spices. As its name imples, alchermes was brought to Europe by the Arabs (*qirmiz* is Arabic for red). It arrived in Tuscany via Spain, and has been made there by the monks of S. Maria Novella in Florence for many centuries. Its colour originally came from the dried, pulverized bodies of a scale insect, *Coccus ilicis*, which is a parasite on an ilex (or evergreen) oak, the kermes oak. Kermès was widely used as a food colouring in the medieval period and was also used for the red colouring of the liqueur Kermès. This survives in France and Italy, but nowadays the colour is more likely to be obtained from cochineal. The principal use of alchermes is for *zuppa inglese* and other soft puddings.

ALMONDS, usually in flaked form, are often used as a decoration for trifles but especially for making the 'spines' on hedgehog tipsy cakes.

AMARETTO (di Saronno) is an almond-flavoured liqueur named after the town of Saronno in Italy where it is made. See also MACAROON for amaretti, the biscuits.

ANGELICA, the candied stalk of the umbelliferous plant *Angelica archangelica*, is a decoration commonly used for cakes and trifles. Growing and candying angelica have been a speciality of Niort in France since the latter part of the eighteenth century.

BOUDOIR BISCUITS are in effect the same as sponge biscuits or sponge fingers, ladyfingers (N. America) and Naples or Savoy (or Savoiardi) biscuits (an older term). They are long, finger-shaped, crisp sponge biscuits based on whisked egg-and-sugar mixtures with a crystallized sugar topping. In France they are also called *biscuits à la cuiller*.
    Although boudoir entered the English language from French long ago and its application to these biscuits could therefore have arisen in England, it seems clear that the French were the first to use the name. Boudoir comes from the French verb *bouder*, to pout, and normally refers to a woman's private room where she would receive only her intimate friends – who could

pout and nibble sponge fingers as much as they wished in this cloistered environment. 'Boudoir' is often embossed on the bottom of the biscuits.

CANDIED (OR CRYSTALLIZED) PEEL OR FRUIT (orange, lemon and citron) are fruits preserved by soaking in syrup for several days until the sugar replaces the moisture in the fruit. The result is very sweet and firm-textured, retaining the shape, and usually the colour, of the original.

CANDIED (OR CYRSTALLIZED) VIOLETS AND ROSE PETALS, are flowers and petals preserved by a coating of sugar syrup. Hot syrup is poured over the fresh flowers, and stirred until the sugar 'grains' or recrystallizes. This method was also applied to orange flowers in the past. Almonds and orange peel were also treated this way, and the results of such recipes were referred to as pralines. Candied violets are still made commercially at Toulouse in France, where they are known as *violettes de Toulouse*.

A simpler technique, used by home cooks, is to brush flower petals with egg white or gum arabic solution, and then dredge them with caster sugar. The principal use of candied flowers in modern times is as decoration for chocolates, cakes or trifles.

CAPIROTADA, a name used in medieval Spain for a sauce for meat, or a dish of meat and sauce, but in modern Mexico it is a Lent pudding, eaten all over the country in different forms. In its most common modern version it looks like a bread pudding without custard. It is soaked with 'piloncillo' (dark brown unrefined sugar) syrup, and has cinnamon, almonds/peanuts, raisins and grated cheese. There is even a tripe capirotada and in the State of Colima, they add onions. The name capirotada can even be used as a name for a Mexican trifle. An example is Capirotada 'San Marcos' a dessert attributed to Aguascalientes, a state in the central highlands of Mexico. This dish is very similar to the recipe *Ante de Yemas* on page 75.

CHAFINGDISH, a portable brazier to hold burning coals or charcoal and designed to be set on a metal stand. Dishes of food could be finished or reheated over this, away from the fierce heat of the hearth.

CHANTILLY CREAM, known in France as *crème Chantilly*, is a sweetened and often flavoured (usually with vanilla) whipped cream, used in many desserts. It is a common topping for trifles or tipsy cakes. Mrs Rundell (1806) has a recipe for 'Chantilly cake' or cake trifle, see page 31. Use of the name Chantilly may have arisen because the famous French château at Chantilly had become a symbol of refined food, of which *crème Chantilly* is a fine example.

COMFIT, an archaic English word for an item of confectionery consisting of a seed or nut coated in several layers of sugar, equivalent to the French DRAGÉE. In England these small, hard sugar sweets were often made with caraway seeds, known for sweetening the breath (hence 'kissing comfits'). Up to a dozen coats of syrup were needed before the seeds were satisfactorily encrusted. Comfits were eaten as sweets, and also used in sweet dishes.

The word comfit remained in use in English up until the twentieth century: Alice, of *Alice in Wonderland*, has a box of comfits in her pocket. During the twentieth century, however, it has become obsolete, and the confectionery produced by this method is now known under invididual names, including HUNDREDS AND THOUSANDS which in turn were sometimes known as 'harlequin' comfits.

CUSTARD, a mixture of milk (or cream) and eggs, sweetened and flavoured for use in desserts, and thickened by gentle heating. Flavours commonly used include vanilla, lemon and almond.

Custard sauce (or *crème anglaise*, as it is sometimes called) is made from the same ingredients as custard, but is runnier and is not normally used for trifles.

Custard powder was invented in the 1830s by Alfred Bird who experimented in making a custard without eggs, to which his wife was allergic. It consists mainly of cornflour, coloured and flavoured, to which hot milk is added to make a sauce.

DRAGÉE, the French name for a sweetmeat composed of a nut or some other centre coated with layers of hard sugar. Almonds are the nuts usually chosen, although seeds, fruit pastes or chocolate are sometimes used. See also COMFITS and HUNDREDS AND THOUSANDS.

FLOATING ISLAND, a cold dessert consisting of a round, flattish, baked meringue 'island' floating on a sea of CUSTARD. In France a similar dish is called *Ile flottante*. Another French dish called *Oeufs à la neige* ('snow eggs' – see also page 89) is made by forming beaten egg whites into small rounds (not one large one) which are then poached and placed on top of a light egg custard or trifle. In either case the islands may be topped with caramel or grated almond or the like.

Hannah Glasse (1747) seems to be the earliest English reference in print. She calls it Flooting Island and her islands were being made with thin slices of French rolls, plus jam or jelly, rather than meringue. See page 19.

Marian McNeill (1929) has a Scottish version which is different again; the egg whites are whisked with quince or raspberry jelly then piled on top of cream beaten with wine and sugar and a little lemon peel.

FOOL, for many centuries a popular British dessert, is now a simple mixture of mashed fruit, raw or cooked as appropriate, with whipped cream. It is particularly suited to being made with acid northern fruits: gooseberries, raspberries, rhubarb, damsons, etc.

The name 'fool' is thought to be derived from the French *fouler* (to mash). So it is reasonable to suppose that the idea of mashed fruit was there from the start. However, one of the earliest fools, Norfolk fool, popular during the seventeenth century, contained no fruit. It was a rich boiled custard made with cream, eggs, sugar, and spices. It could be called 'Devonshire whitepot', Devon being a principal dairy farming county. See WHITE POTS.

GÉNOISE CAKE, a type of sponge cake (which may be called Génoise, in Britain, but should not be confused with Genoa cake, which is a sort of light fruit cake). Whole eggs are beaten with sugar until thick, and then the flour is folded in. Génoise-type mixtures are also made into sponge fingers – see BOUDOIR BISCUITS and SAVOY.

GLACÉ FRUITS, especially cherries but also pineapple, are common decorations for trifle. See also CANDIED FRUITS.

HARTSHORN JELLY, a JELLY made from the shavings of the antlers of a hart (i.e. stag) used in cooking in the seventeenth and eighteenth centuries. Hannah Glasse calls for hartshorn jelly in her recipe for 'Flooting Island', see page 19.

HUNDREDS AND THOUSANDS are tiny DRAGÉES, made by coating individual sugar crystals with sugar syrup. A characteristic of hundreds and thousands is the bright mixture of colours – red, orange, pink, yellow – in which they are produced. These little sweets are scattered over icing to decorate cakes, trifles or sprinkled over ice creams.

The corresponding French term, *nonpareille*, sometimes occurs in the anglicized and archaic form non pareil. They can also go under the name of 'harlequin comfits', see COMFITS.

ISINGLASS is a substance consisting of collagen, which, when heated with water, yields a pure form of gelatin. It is obtained from the swimming bladder (or 'sound') of certain fish, especially the sturgeon, after it has been cleaned, dried and treated. The main use of isinglass has been for clarifying liquids but it is also important for use in confectionery and desserts such as fruit jellies and blancmange. Its use has now been largely superseded for most purposes by leaf, sheet, or powdered gelatin obtained from the collagen which is present in animal bones, skin etc.

JELLY, a dessert made from fruit syrup and gelatin, allowed to set in a cool place. Valued for its clear, sparkling appearance, it was originally based on a gelatin-rich stock made from calves feet (or, sometimes, HARTSHORN or ISINGLASS). This type of jelly demanded time and technical skill during preparation. Eighteenth-century jellies were served in glasses, sometimes presented as 'ribbons' – layers of jelly in different colours. Nineteenth-century jellies were often set in elaborate copper moulds, giving tall castellated and other shapes when turned out. For this and much besides, see a brilliant essay by Peter Brears in *PPC* 53 and 54. For the controversial aspect of using jelly in trifles, see page 64.

LADY FINGERS, see BOUDOIR BISCUITS.

LAUREL leaves (normally taken to mean leaves of *Laurocerasus officinalis*, the cherry laurel) may sometimes be used, but only in minuscule quantity, for flavouring CUSTARDS etc. When a recipe specifies laurel leaves, it may be because the author is aware of this and means what he says. But more often it is a mistake for 'bay leaves', from *L. nobilis*. The French word *laurier* means bay leaf, and this can cause confusion.

MACAROONS are small round biscuit-like confections composed of sweet almonds, finely chopped or ground, mixed with sugar and beaten egg whites and baked lightly. Macaroon recipes have appeared in cookery books since at least the late seventeenth century. RATAFIAS are similar but are usually smaller and contain a proportion of bitter almonds.

Macaroons were often served with wine or liqueurs as a light refreshment in the eighteenth and nineteenth centuries. They were also used in cookery, to provide texture and flavour in desserts and cakes. Typically, they were crushed and used in trifles; and used whole, as decorations and accompaniments for creams and SYLLABUBS. Almond macaroons are still used in this way.

Amaretti are small Italian almond biscuits, typically flavoured with bitter almonds or apricot kernels.

MADEIRA wine and cake. Madeira cake is often used as the cake base for a trifle and Madeira, a fortified wine, was often used to soak this cake (or biscuit) layer. The cake is a rich one, flavoured with lemon zest and decorated with a thin slice of candied citron; some recipes are similar to pound cake. Jane Grigson (1974) remarks that the cake 'was served with Madeira and other sweet wines in the nineteenth century, hence the name.'

MALAGA, a fortified wine from Malaga in Spain, sometimes used to soak the biscuit or cake layer of a trifle.

MAMEY, the Spanish (and Mexican) name of a fruit native to the W. Indies,

Mammea americana, which is now cultivated throughout tropical America. It is a round fruit the size of an orange or larger with firm pulp which has something of the flavour of an apricot.

MANCHET, a seventeenth-century term meaning a loaf of fine bread.

MARASCHINO a sweet liqueur, originally made in Dalmatia, Yugoslavia, from the wild sour Marasca (or Maraschino) cherry, and is now also made in Italy. The flavour is like that of bitter almonds, produced by crushing the cherry stones. The name is most familiar nowadays in its use for 'Maraschino cherries', preserved in a syrup with the same flavour and coloured red or green.

MARSALA, a golden fortified wine of Sicily made from white and red grapes grown around Marsala and sometimes used to soak the biscuit or cake layer of a trifle.

MATRIMONY CAKES are mentioned in the recipe by Hannah Glasse on page 24. They are a mystery, not soluble by reference to any of the usual sources.

MUTCHKIN, a Scottish measure, about ¾ of an Imperial pint, or to be more correct and up to date, just over 400 ml.

MYRTLE, *Myrtus communis*, a shrub native to the mountain regions of the Mediterranean, has glossy, aromatic leaves and fragrant flowers. Myrtle is used in much the same way as bay for flavouring food, especially with others spices and herbs.

NAPLES BISCUITS, see BOUDOIR BISCUITS.

NONPAREILS, see COMFITS.

NOYEAU (or Noyau) a liqueur made from fruit (apricot, peach, etc.) kernels. *Noyau* is the French term for a kernel.

ORANGE FLOWER WATER, sometimes called orange blossom water, is produced by the distillation of flowers of the bitter orange (also called bigarade or Seville orange). This produces an essential oil called Neroli, which is used in perfumery. The oil, rising to the surface, is drawn off, while the aqueous portion is used as orange flower water.

Orange flower water originated in the Middle East where it is still used. It is often added with rosewater, or on its own, to *atr*, the sugar syrup which is used to soak or sprinkle over pastries and sweets lending them a delicate perfume.

By the seventeenth century, it was widely used in Europe to flavour foods, including custards and creams for trifles.

OSWEGO FLOUR, a proprietary name for a type of cornflour, crops up in certain nineteenth-century recipes.

POUND CAKE, a cake of the creamed type, is so named because the recipe calls for an equal weight of flour, butter, sugar, and eggs; in old recipes, a pound of each, making a large, rich cake which was often used as the base for a trifle or tipsy cake.

Pound cake has been favoured in both Britain and the USA for over two centuries. Recipes for it were already current early in the eighteenth century.

RATAFIA, a word with three meanings, as follows:

(1) Ratafia, a drink popular in the seventeenth and eighteenth centuries, probably of French origin. It was a cordial or a brandy-based liqueur flavoured with almonds, peach, cherry or apricot kernels, or soft fruits; similar to noyau, a word which came into use in the late eighteenth century and largely supplanted ratafia.

(2) Ratafia, an eighteenth- and nineteenth-century variation on the MACAROON, flavoured with bitter almonds (or sometimes with apricot kernels). These biscuits may have acquired the name because they were eaten with the drink ratafia, or because of the use of bitter almonds as a flavouring in both items. Very small almond biscuits are still manufactured under the name of 'ratafias'.

(3) The word is also used to describe a bitter almond flavour; for instance, 'essence of ratafia' (essence of bitter almond); or 'ratafea cream' (a dessert flavoured with apricot kernels – see Mrs Eales, 1718).

RENNET is a substance used for curdling milk, either as part of cheese-making or to make the dessert junket. Most rennet is of animal origin, but vegetable rennet obtained from plants such as the wild cardoon is also available. In the seventeenth century rennet was sometimes used in the making of trifles; see pages 15–18.

ROSEWATER, is a fragrant flavouring obtained by the distillation of rose petals, used as a flavouring for food for many centuries.

Its use spread from the Arab world to Europe via the Crusaders. It was popular in medieval England, where it was used in many desserts, but less popular in more recent times. However, it is still used extensively all over the Indian sub-continent and the Middle East.

SACK, an amber-coloured wine made in southern Spain, was first imported into England during the reign of Henry VIII and enjoyed some popularity until the nineteenth century. It was often used as a flavouring in trifles.

Savoy biscuits/cake (in French *Savoie, biscuit de Savoie*) is a type of light and delicate sponge cake which differs from a génoise in that the egg yolks and whites are beaten separately. Vanilla and lemon are often added as flavourings. The Italian *pan di Spagna* used in Italy for *zuppa inglese* is similar but contains less sugar.

The same mixture is also used to make small biscuits. Savoy biscuits (also called Savoiardi) arrived in England early in the eighteenth century, perhaps helping to pave the way for the development of the modern trifle. Other similar biscuits, named according to their supposed origins – Naples, Lisbon, etc., became popular in England at much the same time. The differences between them, if differences there were, no doubt perplexed people then as they do now. See also boudoir biscuit.

Sherry, a fortified wine made from white grapes in and around the Spanish town of Jerez, has enjoyed particular esteem in Britain for several centuries. It was thus a natural choice for cooks seeking an alcoholic drink to use in trifles; and the phrase 'sherry trifle' is in common use.

Skillet, a term in use from the seventeenth century, refers to a sturdy metal pot, with legs, and a handle. It could be stood right in the fire.

Snow and snow eggs. Snow, a dessert which first became popular in the sixteenth century, was simply a confection of egg whites and cream, flavoured with rosewater and a little sugar and whipped until stiff; or any of a number of variations on this theme. It was sometimes served as a novelty at banquets, mounded over an apple and spread on the twigs of a branch of rosemary to look like real snow. In the eighteenth century cooked apple pulp was added to make apple snow. This dish, still current, is now a light egg white and apple pureé mixture, to be eaten cold and sometimes used as a topping for trifles – see page 45. See also pages 89–90 for 'snow egg' topping and egg-snow trifle.

Sponge fingers, see Boudoir biscuits.

Syllabub (or sillabub) is a sweet, frothy confection which was popular in Britain from the sixteenth to the nineteenth century, and has since been revived in a small way as a dessert. The origin of the word 'syllabub' is a mystery. Lexicographers find no compelling reason to accept any of the explanations offered so far.

Originally syllabub was a drink with a foamy head, but the foamy part was the object of chief interest and later became the main element. It was this which was set to drain and then used as a topping for trifles. Ivan Day (1996) provides a historical and technical survey of the whole subject of syllabubs, now the *locus classicus*. See also page 95.

TIFFANY was a seventeenth-century term for a kind of fine transparent silk or lawn used as a mesh for sieving and straining. A muslin cloth is now more commonly used.

TRIFLE LEAVES. We think that trifle leaves (referred to in Mrs Leyel's trifle recipe – see page 44) must be the same as what are also called chocolate leaves which are often used for decorating trifles and cakes. They are made by coating the underside of fresh rose leaves with melted chocolate; and then, when the chocolate has set or hardened, the rose leaf is carefully peeled off and discarded.

WHITE POTS, together with trifles and FOOLS, were among the dishes using cream which became increasingly popular during Tudor and Stuart periods. The cream might be thickened with breadcrumbs (or rice) as well as egg and often contained currants and was flavoured with ROSEWATER or nutmeg etc. It was then boiled or baked in a pot or pan, hence the name.

BIBLIOGRAPHY

The place of publication is London, unless otherwise indicated.
PPC refers to the food history journal *Petits Propos Culinaires* (Prospect Books, from 1979 onwards).

Acton, Eliza, *Modern Cookery for Private Families*, Longman, Green, Longman and Roberts, 1860

Allen, Brigid, *Food, An Oxford Anthology*, Oxford University Press, Oxford, 1994

Allen, Myrtle, *The Ballymaloe Cookbook*, 3rd edn., Gill and Macmillan, Dublin, 1987

Ayto, John, *The Diner's Dictionary*, Oxford University Press, Oxford, 1993

Bacon, Josephine, *Pâtisserie of Vienna*, Macdonald Orbis, 1988

Bain, Priscilla, 'Recounting the Chickens: Hannah Further Scrutinized' in *PPC* 23, 1986

Barossa Cookery Book, 27th edn. (first published *c.* 1917, Tanunda, S. Australia, *c.* 1980

Beeton, Mrs Isabella, *Mrs Beeton's Book of Household Management*, S. O. Beeton, 1861

Bracken, Peg, *Appendix to the I Hate to Cook Book*, Fawcett Publication, Greenwich, Conn., 1967

Bradley, Martha, *The British Housewife* (*c.* 1758), facsimile edn., vols i-vi, , Prospect Books, Totnes, 1996–8

Brears, Peter, 'Transparent Pleasures – the Story of the Jelly': Part One and Part Two in *PPC* 53 and 54, 1996

Brooks, Shirley Lomax, *Argentina Cooks!*, Hippocrene Books, New York, 2001

Brown, Catherine, *Scottish Cookery*, Richard Drew, Glasgow, 1985

Burton, David, *Two Hundred Years of New Zealand Food and Cookery*, Reed, Wellington, 1982

Byron, May, *May Byron's Pudding Book*, Hodder and Stoughton, 1923

Byron, May, *Pot Luck*, Hodder and Stoughton, 1914

Caruana Galizia, Anne and Helen, *The Food & Cookery of Malta*, Prospect Books, Totnes, 1997

Chamberlain, Lesley, In 'Notes and Queries', *PPC* 51, 1995

Cleland, Elizabeth, *A New and Easy Method of Cookery*, Edinburgh, 1755

Cookery Book of Good and Tried Receipts, 12th edn., Sydney, 1912

Cooper, Jos, *the art of cookery refin'd*, 1654

Cox, Helen, *Traditional English Cooking*, Angus and Robertson, 1961

Craig, Elizabeth, *The Stage Favourites Cook Book*, Hutchinson, 1923

Craig, Elizabeth , *Court Favourites*, Andre Deutsch, 1953

Cre-Fydd, *Cre-Fydd's Family Fare: The Young Housewife's Daily Assistant*, Simpkin, Marshall, 1866

Dalgairns, Mrs, *Practice of Cookery*, 2nd edn., printed for Cadell & Company, Edinburgh, 1829

David, Elizabeth, *An Omelette and a Glass of Wine*, Robert Hale – A Jill Norman Book, 1984

Davidson, Alan, *The Oxford Companion to Food*, Oxford University Press, Oxford, 1999

Dawson, Thomas, *The Good Huswifes Jewell*, Parts 1 and 2, (repr. as a single volume, Theatrum Orbis Terrarum, Amsterdam, 1977), 1596, 1597

Dawson, Thomas, *The Good Housewife's Jewel* (new edn., with added matter, of the preceding item), Southover Press, Lewes, 1996

Day, Ivan, 'Further Musings on Syllabub, ...', in *PPC* 53, 1996

de Leon, Josefina Velazquez, *Mexican Cook Book Devoted to American Homes*, 11th edn., Culinary Arts Institute, Mexico City, 1978

de Salis, Mrs, *A La Mode Cookery*, Longmans, Green, 1902

Del Conte, Anna, *Gastronomy of Italy*, Prentice Hall Press, New York, 1987

Dewitt, Dave and Wilan, Mary Jane, *Callaloo, Calypso and Carnival*, The Crossing Press, Freedom, Ca., 1993

Dods, Mistress Margaret (Meg), *The Cook and Housewife's Manual*, 15th edn., Oliver and Boyd, Edinburgh, c. 1883

Donati, William, *Ida Lupino – A Biography*, University Press of Kentucky, Kentucky?, 1996

Driver, Elizabeth, *A Bibliography of Cookery Books Published in Britain 1875–1914*, Prospect Books, 1989

Duckitt, Hildagonda J., *Hilda's "Where Is It?" of Recipes,* Seventh Thousand, Chapman and Hall, 1895

Eales, Mrs Mary, *Mrs. Mary Eales's Receipts* (1718), facsimile reprint (of 1733 edition), Prospect Books, 1985

Evelyn, John (ed Christopher Driver), *John Evelyn, Cook*, Prospect Books, Devon, 1997

Family Receipt-Book, Oddy and Oddy, nd (?1810)

Fisher, M.F.K., *With Bold Knife and Fork*, G.P. Putnam's & Sons, New York, 1968/69

Florio, John, *First Fruites. Also a perfect induction to the Italian, and English tongues*, London, 1578 (reprinted, Theatrum Orbis Terrarum, Amsterdam, 1969)

For Home Use, 8th edn., Angostura Bitters (Dr J.G.B. Siegert & Sons), Port of Spain, 1937

Frazer, Mrs, *The Practice of Cookery, Pastry, Confectionary ...* , 2nd edn., printed for Peter Hill etc., Edinburgh, 1795

Garrett, Theodore Francis, *The Encyclopaedia of Practical Cookery*, Upcott Gill, *c.* 1895

[Glasse, Hannah], *The Art of Cookery Made Plain and Easy*, by 'A Lady' (facsimile reprint Prospect Books, Totnes, 1995), 1747

[Glasse, Hannah], *The Art of Cookery Made Plain and Easy*, by 'A Lady', 4th edn., 1751

Glasse, Hannah, *The Compleat Confectioner, c.* 1760

Goodwin, Betty, *Hollywood du Jour – Lost Recipes of Legendary Hollywood Haunts*, Angel City Press, Santa Monica, 1993

Gosetti, Fernanda, *I Dolci della cucina regionale italiana*, Fabbri Editore, Milano, 1993

Gouffé, Jules, *Le livre de Pâtisserie*, Hachette, Paris, 1873

Grigson, Jane, *English Food*, Macmillan, 1974

Grigson, Jane, *Jane Grigson's Fruit Book*, Michael Joseph, 1982

Grigson, Jane, *Cooking of the Mediterranean – A Sainsbury Cookbook*, Martin Books, 1991

Hagdahl, Dr Ch. Em., *Kok-konsten* (Arts of Cookery), edn. of 1896, reprinted in facsimile, Gastronomiska Akademiens Bibliotek, 1963

Harland, Marion, *Marion Harland's Complete Cook Book*, The Bobbs-Merrill Company, Indianapolis, 1903

Hess, Karen (ed), *Martha Washington's Booke of Cookery*, Columbia University Press, New York, 1981

Hill, Annabella P., *Mrs. Hill's Southern Practical Cookery and Receipt Book* (1872), facsimile reprint, University of South Carolina Press, Columbia SC, 1995

Hopkins, Martha and Lockridge, Randall, *Inter Courses: an aphrodisiac cookbook* , Hamlyn, 1997

Hutchins, Sheila, *English Recipes and Others from Scotland, Wales and Ireland*, Methuen, 1967

Jones, Lucy, *Puddings and Sweets*, Henry S. King, 1877

Kaneva-Johnson, *The Melting Pot: Balkan Food and Cookery* , Prospect Books, Totnes, 1995

Kenney-Herbert, Colonel A.R., *Culinary Jottings for Madras by "Wyvern"* [fifth edition] (Madras, 1885), facsimile reprint, Prospect Books, Totnes, 1994

Kirk, Mrs E.W., *Tried Favourites Cookery Book*, Horace Marshall, 1948

Ladies of Toronto, The, *The New Cook Book*, rev edn., Rose Publishing, Toronto, 1906

Lady's Companion, vols I and II, 4th edn., printed for T. Read and Baldwin, 1743

Lady's Companion, vols I and II, 5th edn., printed for T. Read and R. Baldwin, 1751

Lang, George, *The Cuisine of Hungary,* Bonanza Book, New York, 1971

Leyel, Mrs C.F, *Puddings,* George Routledge & Sons, nd

Lucraft, Fiona, 'A Study of the *Compleat Confectioner* by Hannah Glasse (c 1760)', Parts One, Two and Three in *PPC* 56, 57 and 58, 1997, 1998

Maciver, Susannah, *Cookery and Pastry,* new edn., printed for C. Eliot, Edinburgh, 1787

Maclean, Virginia, *A Short-title Catalogue of Household and Cookery Books Published in the English Tongue 1701–1800,* Prospect Books, 1981

Magazine of Domestic Economy, Vol 4, W.S. Orr & Co, 1839

Mangor, A.M, *Kogebog for Maa Huusholdninger* (A cook book for small households), 6th edn., Copenhagen, 1844

Mariani, John, *The Dictionary of Italian Food and Drink,* Broadway Books, New York, 1998

Mason, Sarah, *The New Experienced English House-keeper,* Doncaster, 1795

Massey & Sons, *The Comprehensive Pudding Book,* 4th edn., Simpkin, Marshall, c. 1875

May, Robert, *The Accomplisht Cook* (1685). facsimile reprint, Prospect Books, Totnes, 1994

McNeill, Marian, *The Scots Kitchen,* Blackie, Glasgow, 1929 (facsimile reprint, Mercat Press, Edinburgh)

McNeill, Marian, *The Scots Kitchen,* 2nd edn., Blackie & Son, Glasgow, 1963

More Favourite Puddings of Rural England, compiled by the editor of *Favourite Puddings of Rural England,* The Cable Printing and Publishing Co, nd (?1930s)

Norwak, Mary, *English Puddings: Sweet and Savoury,* B. T. Batsford, 1981

Notaker, Henry, 'A Taste of Norway', Royal Norwegian Ministry of Foreign Affairs, 1996

Ortiz, Elisabeth Lambert, *The Complete Book of Mexican Cooking,* M. Evans, New York, 1967

Patten, Marguerite, *Learning to Cook,* Phoenix House, 1955

Petty, Florence, *The 'Pudding Lady's' Recipe Book,* G. Bell, 1917

Porrua, Miguel Angel (Ed), *Nuevo Cocinero Mexicano en forma de Diccionario* (1888) facsimile reprint, Mexico, 1986

Raffald, Elizabeth, *The Experienced English Housekeeper,* 3rd edn., 1773

Randolph, Mary, *The Virginia Housewife* (historical notes and commentaries by Karen Hess), facsim. of the 1st edn. of 1824 with additional material from edn. 1825 and 1828, Univ. of South Carolina Press, Columbia, 1984

Rhett, Blanche; Gay, Lettie and Woodward, Helen, *200 Years of Charleston Cooking,* rev edn. , Random House, New York, 1934

Rhodes, Dennis (ed), *In An Eighteenth Century Kitchen – A Receipt Book of Cookery 1698*, Cecil and Amelia Woolf, 1968

Richardson, Louise A. and Isabell, J.R., 'Joseph Cooper, Chief Cook to Charles I' in *PPC* 18, 1984

Riddell, Dr R, *Indian Domestic Economy,* Thacker, Spink and Co, Calcutta, 1871

Rögnvaldardóttir, Nanna, *Icelandic Food and Cookery*, Hippocrene Books, New York, 2001

Roundell, Mrs, *Mrs Roundell's Practical Cookery Book*, Bickers & Son, 1898

[Rundell, Mrs], *A New System of Domestic Cookery, by 'A Lady'*, printed for J. Murray, 1806

[Rundell, Mrs], *A New System of Domestic Cookery*, new edn., John Murray, 1842

Rutledge, Anna Wells, *The Carolina Housewife* (1847), facsimile reprint, University of South Carolina Press, Columbia, SC, 1979

Sabban, F. and Serventi, S., Contribution to 'Notes and Queries', *PPC* 51, 1995

Saberi, Helen, *Noshe Djan – Afghan Food and Cookery*, rev. edn., Prospect Books, Totnes, 2000

Saberi, Helen, 'Whims and Fancies of a Trifle Lover', in *PPC* 50, 1995

Schneider, Elizabeth, *Uncommon Fruits and Vegetables*, Harper and Row, New York, 1986 and 2000

Sheridan, Monica, *My Irish Cook Book*, Frederick Muller, 1965

Sing, Phia, *Traditional Recipes of Laos*, Prospect Books, 1981

Stead, Jennifer, 'Quizzing Glasse: Or Hannah Scrutinized', Parts 1 and 2 in *PPC* 13 and 14, 1983

Veal, Irene, *Anthology of Puddings*, John Gifford, 1942

Veldsman, Peter, *The Flavours of South Africa*, Tafelberg, 1998

Warren, Olivia, *Taste of Eritrea*, Hippocrene, New York, 2000

White, Florence, *Good Things in England*, Jonathan Cape, 1932

Wilson, C. Anne, *Food and Drink in Britain from the Stone Age to Recent Times,* Cookery Book Club, 1973

Wiseman, Shelton & others, *The Mexican Gourmet,* Thunder Bay Press, Mexico, 1995

Women's Institute and Michael Smith, *A Cook's Tour of Britain*, Willow Books, 1984

Wolley (Woolley), Hannah, *The Queen-like Closet*: 5th edn., 1684

MEASURES: TABLES OF EQUIVALENCE

This book does not require comprehensive tables of equivalence, since the specialized nature of its subject limits the numbers of measures employed. The simple and short tables of equivalence which follow below should be sufficient.

However, these tables must be prefaced by some remarks about old measures, especially liquid measures in pre-1864 recipes such as may be found in Chapters One and Two and the first half of Chapter Three. In 1864 the British (imperial) pint was redefined as being 20 fl. oz. However, the change was ignored in North America, where a pint continued to be 16 fl. oz. This divergence, as Tom Stobart remarks in his admirable *Cook's Encyclopaedia*, 'has had British and American cooks, publishers and food manufacturers swearing ever since'. Stobart further points out that the British fluid ounce is fractionally smaller than the American fluid ounce (they are 28.4 ml and 29.6 ml respectively) but this additional discrepancy is too trifling to need attention from trifle makers.

So, in using a British recipe earlier than 1864, assume that a pint means an American pint (see Table Three below). If an old recipe refers to a gill, that may be taken to mean ¼ of an American pint, and a quart equalled 2 American pints. One or two other ancient and obsolete measures are explained where they occur in the text.

Perfectionists will wish to be reminded that a teaspoon seems to have been a larger measure in the eighteenth century, when its main use was for measuring rather than stirring, than it is now.

Finally, a note for Canadian, Australian and New Zealand readers. As you no doubt know, your pints are imperial (British), but your measuring cups are – or have been until converted to metric – American.

Table One: Weights

metric	British/U.S.	metric	British/U.S.
10 g	0.36 oz	340 g	12.0 oz (¾ lb)
28 g	1.0 oz	454 g	16.0 oz (1 lb)
50 g	1.8 oz	500 g (½ kg)	1 lb 1.8 oz
56 g	2.0 oz	567 g	1¼ lb
100 g	3.6 oz	675 g	1½ lb
113 g	4.0 oz (¼ lb)	750 g (¾ kg)	1 lb 10.7 oz
150 g	5.3 oz	908 g	2 lb
227 g	8.0 oz (½ lb)	1 kg	2 lb 3.7 oz
250 g (¼ kg)	8.9 oz		

Table Two: Measures of Capacity
(equivalences between fluid ounces and millilitres)

metric (ml)	British fl. oz.	metric (ml)	British fl. oz.
5 (1 tsp)	0.18	227	8
15 (1 tbs)	0.5	250 (¼ litre)	8.9
28	1	280	10
30 (2 tbs)	1.1	336	12
45 (3 tbs)	1.6	392	14
56	2	454	16
60 (4 tbs)	2.1	500 (½ litre)	17.9
84	3	600	21.4
98	3.5	750 (¾ litre)	26.8
112	4	896	32
125	4.5	1 litre	35.7
150	5.4	1 ½ litres	53.6
196	7	2 litres	71.4

Table Three: Further Measures of Capacity
(for cooks accustomed to using pints and cups)

British	American	fl.. oz.	metric (ml)
	¼ cup	2	57
¼ cup		2.5	71
	⅓ cup	2.7	76
⅓ cup		3.3	95
	½ cup (¼ pint)	4	113
½ cup (¼ pint)		5	142
	⅔ cup	5.3	151
⅔ cup		6.7	189
	¾ cup	6	170
¾ cup		7.5	198
	1 cup (½ pint)	8	227
1 cup (½ pint)		10	284
	2 cups (1 pint)	16	454
2 cups (1 pint)		20	567
	3 cups	24	680
3 cups		30	850
	4 cups (2 pints)	32	907
4 cups (2 pints		40	1134

NOTES

NOTES

A VALEDICTORY VERSE

TRIFLE

Air – "The Meeting of the Waters"

There's not in the wide world so tempting a sweet
As that Trifle where custard and macaroons meet;
Oh ! the latest sweet tooth from my head must depart
Ere the taste of that Trifle shall not win my heart.

Yet it is not the sugar that's thrown in between
Nor the peel of the lemon so candied and green;
'Tis not the rich cream that's whipp'd up by a mill:
Oh, no ! it is something more exquisite still.

'Tis that nice macaroons in the dish I have laid,
Of which a delicious foundation is made;
And you'll find how the last will in flavour improve.
When soak'd with the wine that you pour in above.

Sweet *plateau* of Trifle ! how great is my zest
For thee, when spread o'er with the jam I love best;
When the cream white of eggs – to be over thee thrown.
With a whisk kept on purpose – is mingled in one !

(From *Punch* (*circa* 1860), quoted in *Food for Thought: An anthology of Writings Inspired by Food,* ed. Joan and John Digby (New York, 1987) page 446.